The Edge of Home:
Milton Acorn from the Island

Poems selected by
Anne Compton
With a Preface and Introduction

ISLAND STUDIES PRESS
INSTITUTE OF ISLAND STUDIES
Charlottetown
2002

ISBN 0-919013-35-X

Cover image *Portrait of Milton Acorn, 1986*, by Brian Burke, from a Private Collection
Cover photography by Kate Kechnie
Design by UPEI Graphics
Printing by Williams & Crue, Summerside, PE Canada

The Institute of Island Studies gratefully acknowledges funding support from the Cultural Development Program of the Prince Edward Island Department of Community and Cultural Affairs.

Special thanks go to Brian Burke, Judith Scherer-Burke, Kevin Rice, Roberta Lloyd, and Kate Kechnie for their assistance with the cover painting; Mary Hooper, Katherine Traynor, and Robert Acorn for supporting the project from the beginning and for giving us permission to use the poems; and to the Institute of Island Studies Publishing Committee, whose good judgement and editorial guidance have steered us well.

National Library of Canada Cataloguing in Publication Data

Acorn, Milton, 1923–1986
    The Edge of Home: Milton Acorn from the Island

ISBN 0-919013-35-X

    1. Prince Edward Island — Poetry. I. Compton, Anne.
II. University of Prince Edward Island. Institute of Island Studies.
III. Title.

PS8501.C8A6 2002   C811'.54   C2001-903319-2
PR9199.3.A18A6 2002

ISLAND STUDIES PRESS
Institute of Island Studies
University of Prince Edward Island
Charlottetown, PE Canada C1A 4P3
tel: (902)566-0956
fax: (902)566-0756
e-mail: iis@upei.ca
website: www.islandstudies.com

For Milton Acorn

Contents

Acknowledgements

In writing the Preface and Introduction, I relied upon the several biographers and many critics who have written about Milton Acorn's life and work. I am especially indebted to D. M. R. Bentley whose work *The Gay] Grey Moose: Essays on the Ecologies and Mythologies of Canadian Poetry 1690–1990* provided a model for my essay, "The Ecological Poetics of Milton Acorn's Island Poems." Richard Lemm, author of *Milton Acorn: In Love and Anger*, generously assisted with the biographical note, and John Smith, scholar and poet, commented — with his usual perceptiveness and insight — on an early version of the manuscript. I am grateful to George Elliott Clarke with whom I have had many wonderful conversations about Milton Acorn. To him and to other poets — among them Frank Ledwell, Richard Lemm, John MacKenzie, and Joseph Sherman — who have written poems honouring Milton Acorn, my thanks for your inspiration.

Laurie Brinklow, Publishing Co-ordinator at the Institute of Island Studies, patiently and gracefully endured my procrastination on this project. For this, and for her attentive editing, thank you.

I dedicate these labours to the memory of my brother, my childhood playmate, John Grant Compton.

Wherever you are be fearless….
M.A.

Milton Acorn: a brief biographical note

To these qualities he has added a disposition to be affected more than other men by absent things as if they were present....
— William Wordsworth

Milton Acorn has few, if any, descendants in poetry. Even those who share his birthplace, Prince Edward Island, cannot match, although they admire, his singular gift for expressing the Island in verse. The "Natural History" of his kind is one entry long. A brutal talker and a tireless scribbler, he was fiercely proud of his place of origin and fierce in his politics. Although the Island was at the centre of his Canada, according to some accounts, he was at the centre of literary and cultural developments in Canada from 1955 to 1980. For some, he was an *historical force*. Still, no one says of this or that emerging poet, "he is like Milton Acorn."

The eldest son of Helen Carbonell and Robert Acorn, James Milton Rhodes Acorn was born in Charlottetown on 30 March 1923. One of five children — three sisters and a brother — Acorn grew up in a close-knit, modestly prosperous family. The extended Island family lived as far east as Murray River and as far west as Summerside. Outside the family circle, Acorn was a solitary, and preoccupied, schoolboy. The familial tradition of storytelling encouraged the avid reader, the imaginative dreamer, who acquired the habit of talking to himself. That oddity, combined with his scrawny boyhood build, provoked neighbourhood bullies. Bluster was the protective garment he wore early, and wore long. At the age of eighteen, Acorn enlisted in the army. On a troopship bound for Europe, he suffered an injury: a blast (of indeterminate origins) inflicted inner ear damage and hearing loss. Surgery and medicines may have complicated the injury.

In the decade following his discharge, Acorn's varied employment included clerking in Moncton and carpentry on the Island. In an interview, some forty years later, Acorn attributed his departure from home to the "reactionary" climate of the 1940s that effectively banned union activity on the Island, a situation intolerable to the would-be "revolutionary" (Burrill 4). He left in 1951. The move to Montreal, and later to cities further west, only confirmed the Island's hold on him. Establishing temporary bases of poetic and political activity in Montreal, Toronto, Vancouver, and then Toronto again, Acorn's return passage was inked into every Island poem he wrote.

In Montreal, he joined the Labour Progressive Party (LPP), kept company with other socialists, and sought out fellow-poets. His first published poem, "Grey Girl's Gallop," a political allegory, appeared in the left-wing periodical *New Frontiers* in 1953. Politics, poetry, and poverty were recurring themes in the letters home. A veteran's disability pension, beginning around 1958, ameliorated the poverty. In poetry, his associates were Al Purdy, Irving Layton, and, on occasion, Leonard Cohen; influences, by his own account, were diverse — from the metaphysical-modernist A. J. M. Smith to the socialist Dorothy Livesay, including the poet who mediated those positions, F. R. Scott. "East Coast, influenced by Scott and Smith along the way," is how Acorn described his poetic lineage (qtd. in Lemm 135). In 1956, he self-published the chapbook *In Love and Anger*. The same year, he left the LPP. This was the pattern of his life: Acorn was a joiner and a quitter. No organization could contain what Al Purdy describes as Acorn's "ferocious...humanism" (Purdy 16). Poetry was the only political forum that claimed his enduring loyalty. In a voice sometimes oracular, sometimes choleric, he inveighed in verse against the shortcomings of political, economic, and social structures, including those of his home province.

The Island poems, among them "I've Tasted My Blood," that he wrote in Montreal in the late 1950s are vivid in physical detail, passionate in their politics. The beauty he saw in persons and places cried out for the preservation of poetry; infringements on that beauty called for "anger, / and often even my forgiveness...."

In 1959, Acorn and Al Purdy were partners in establishing the poetry magazine *Moment*. The next year, with Purdy's help, Acorn published *The Brain's the Target*. Fifteen poems excluded from that volume appeared, the same year, in the broadsheet *Against a League of Liars*. By the early 1960s, he had made the move to Toronto, where he was a raucous, some might say an unruly, force on the Toronto literary scene. At the Bohemian Embassy, the Toronto gathering place of artists, musicians, and writers, Acorn was something of a "poet laureate" (Longfellow). In 1962, he married the brilliant young poet Gwendolyn MacEwen, a union of short duration. For Acorn, a destructive year of despair, and hospitalization, followed the break-up. At the end of it, he would head for Vancouver. But 1963 was also the year that Contact Press published *Jawbreakers* and Fred Cogswell, editor of *The Fiddlehead*, showcased Acorn's work in a special edition of the journal. According to biographer Richard Lemm, "Acorn's inner distress certainly increased from 1962 onward" (136). So did his reputation in literature. The first two books, and the broadsheet, contained the poems around which Acorn would shape the later award-winning collections *I've Tasted My Blood* (1969) and *The Island Means Minago* (1975).

In Vancouver, Acorn participated in the early days of *The Georgia Straight*, the newspaper of the Vancouver counterculture. A contributing editor, he was also "one of [its] founders" (qtd. in Lemm 147). He read, and organized readings, at the Advanced Mattress Coffee House. He became friends with poets bill bissett, Red Lane, Patrick Lane, and Pat Lowther. According to his Vancouver acquaintances, for Acorn, this was a period of fragile physical and mental health although he was, at the same time, often on the streets offering succour to the derelict. When they intercepted him "on the spit-grey downtown streets," he mused ironically, "I wonder how they know me."

Back on the East Coast, to which he returned for short stays in the period 1968 to 1972, Acorn's "nervous episode," as he called it, abated (qtd. in MacFarlane 4). Island friendships were restorative and Acorn, by nature resilient, rebounded in the positive critical reception that followed the publication of *I've Tasted My Blood* in 1969. His dynamic readings drew large crowds in Toronto and on the Island. Reviewers fell over themselves to revise earlier appraisals of the poet: comments on the man and his manner, in the earlier estimates, had frequently eclipsed attention to the work. When *I've Tasted My Blood* failed to win a Governor-General's Award, which many believed the book deserved, poets Eli Mandel and Irving Layton raised money for the Canadian Poets' Award and arranged the celebratory evening at Toronto's Grossman's Tavern where the honour was conferred. Thereafter, Acorn was known as the "People's Poet," the inscription on the reverse side of the medallion he received that night.

Coming and going between Toronto and the Island in those years

(1968–72), Acorn visited with family and friends in Charlottetown or stayed, during the summer months, in one of the South Shore cottages loaned to him by friends. In one of those cottages, according to his friend Reg Phelan, Acorn wrote "a fair bit" of *The Island Means Minago* (qtd. in Lemm 178), published in 1975 by NC Press. A distributor of books and pamphlets, NC Press was the publishing arm of the Canadian Liberation Movement (CLM), an organization "devoted to building an independent, socialist Canada," by encouraging workers, farmers, and students in their opposition to "U.S. imperialist control," including the control of Canadian unions. Its aims were set out in the final pages of Acorn's 1972 *More Poems for People*, also published by NC Press, and in *Minago*. From early in the 1970s until 1976, Acorn belonged to the CLM. His friendship with James Deahl, editor of the posthumous collections of Acorn's verse, dates from this period. While in Toronto in the 1970s, Acorn lived at the Waverly Hotel, a residency memorialized in Cedric Smith's song, "On the third floor of the Waverly hotel." With actor-songwriter Cedric Smith, Acorn wrote *The Road to Charlottetown*, the drama that shares with *Minago* the 19th-century Island story of absentee landlords, a disgruntled tenantry, and the struggle for land ownership. The play was produced at the MacKenzie Theatre in Charlottetown in August and September of 1977 and, in a revised form, in Toronto at Theatre Passe Muraille the next year.

In 1977, Milton Acorn received an honorary degree — a Doctor of Laws, *honoris causa* — from the University of Prince Edward Island. The presenter, John Smith, said that when Milton Acorn writes of the things of this world, "those things become more concrete, more material, and also more alive to us." Smith spoke of Acorn's "poems of faith in the common people," and it was for the "common people" that Acorn, in the same year, published *Jackpine Sonnets*, a collection dedicated to the reassertion of musicality in verse, an aspect of poetry, according to Acorn, abandoned in free verse. The sonnet's "beautiful thought-rhyme," as he referred to it in his introduction, would give poetry back to the people.

In 1981, he returned permanently to the Island: "I know where I am here," he told an interviewer (Burrill 7). The familiar was his point of departure. He would have five years. Ragweed Press published a second sonnet collection, *Captain Neal MacDougal & the Naked Goddess*

(1982), a work loosely based on the life of his grandfather Neil MacDougall, a sea captain. The compass on Neal MacDougal's vessel leads off the map: it is the invisible, not the visible, world that Acorn charts in this next-to-last collection. In 1983, McClelland & Stewart published *Dig Up My Heart: Selected Poems* 1952–83, a selection assembled by Acorn's steadfast friend, Al Purdy. In Charlottetown, and in his visits to the countryside and on his trips to the seashore, Acorn spent his last years with gentle and generous companions, cared for, as he had always been, by a supportive family. This collection is for them as well as for him. He died in 1986. The poems did not.

Works Cited

Burrill, Gary. "An Afternoon with Milton Acorn." *New Maritimes* (May 1984): 4–7.

Lemm, Richard. *Milton Acorn: In Love and Anger*. Ottawa: Carleton UP, 1999.

MacFarlane, David. "The People's Choice." *Books in Canada* (June–July 1981): 3–5.

Purdy, Al. "In Love and Anger." *Books in Canada* (October 1986): 16–18.

Shadow Maker, a documentary. Dir. Brenda Longfellow. Gerda Film, 1998.

The biographical note draws upon interviews; introductions to Acorn's books; information provided by Mary Hooper (Milton Acorn's sister); *Talking Books*, CBC radio, 8 February 1998; poems by Milton Acorn ("Poem with Fat Cats in the Background" and "I've Tasted My Blood"); Rosemary Sullivan's biography of Gwendolyn MacEwen, *Shadow Maker: The Life of Gwendolyn MacEwen*, and Brenda Longfellow's film documentary *Shadow Maker*, based on Sullivan's biography. The chronology of Acorn's life follows the account provided by Richard Lemm in his biography, *Milton Acorn: In Love and Anger*. I am indebted to his fine scholarship.

Preface

The marram grass that grows on Island sand dunes is a deeply rooted, long-stemmed, plant; its sharp leaves will scratch your legs, cut your feet, if you're not careful. Grey-green in colour, it is scarcely distinguishable from the gold-grey of the dune itself. Marram is the coast's protector. Its matted and interwoven root-stocks prevent the drifting of sands and resist the action of waves and winds that wage unceasing warfare on the land. Its value as a sand-binder has long been recognized. Great has been the devastation caused by sand-storms on coasts where the grasses have been removed, as they were from a shore in Scotland in the eighteenth century. During a winter storm, the apple trees, it is said, were buried and only the highest branches showed above the drifts of sand.[1] Centuries later, an Atlantic away, Islanders—recognizing the fragility of this apparently tough plant—take measures to protect the marram.

Like the deeply rooted marram grass, Milton Acorn's poetry — fiercely attached to its place — is the work of a warrior who would shore up the edge of home. To understand more fully the land that lies within the encircling cliffs and dunes, this collection brings together in one volume some of the best of Acorn's PEI poems. "What is the poetic by which he writes 'home'?" and "Who are we in his words?" are a couple of the questions that led to this volume. Perhaps he can tell us: Are we separated from — or connected to — the rest of Canada by water? Reading Acorn, we can know the place *as if* for the first time because he had eyes finer than ours, words more exact.

Mindful of, even preoccupied with, the sea, Acorn leads the reader again and again to the perimeter. Although he moved away in 1951, Acorn never "left" the Island, and he returned permanently in 1981 to live out his last years on the "wave-lined edge of home" and to contemplate anew the sea, the wind, and the horizon that appear in so much of his work. Like the marram grass that edges miles of this most maritime of Maritime provinces, Acorn's poetry is delicate and tough. His poetry is a hedge against what we might let drift away, but for too long its value,

---

[1] I am indebted to two books, from which I borrow liberally, for the information on marram grass: Francis, Mary Evans. *The Book of Grasses: an Illustrated Guide to the Common Grasses, and Most of the Rushes and Sedges. Nature Library.* Vol. XVII. N.Y.: Doubleday and Page, 1912; and MacQuarrie, Kate. *Life at the Edge.* Charlottetown: Island Nature Trust, 1995.

relative to its habitat, has gone unregarded by people like me — expatriate Islanders who want the Island to be just as we left it. Like the character Callum, in the poem of that title, Acorn was "from 'The Island,'" a fact he pronounced proudly, and, although he lived most of his adult years away, he carried the Island landscape with him, within him, carried it "from the Island."

The Edge of Home aspires to recuperate Acorn's Island poems for Islanders. But not only for Islanders. It reaffirms for all readers the importance of the Island in Acorn's work, in all of his work. Since Acorn's death in 1986, James Deahl has brought out seven collections of Acorn's poetry, including *The Uncollected Acorn*, which contains combinations of "different drafts" and reconstructions "of passages in poems" (Introduction n.p.). Like the drifting of sands that follows upon the uprooting of marram grass, this posthumous relocation of Acorn verses obscures the Island that Acorn so carefully discerned, and discerning, preserved.

Two recent biographies — Chris Gudgeon's *Out of This World* (1996) and Richard Lemm's *In Love and Anger* (1999) — have debated the details of the life. The life has been ably told; now it is time for the poetry. As Acorn himself wrote, "a poem erases and rewrites its poet" (68). The poet belongs to the poems. In "Autobiography," Acorn describes the "search" that "invents / and reinvents me" (*Dig Up My Heart: Selected Poems* 1952–83, 187),[2] and, in another poem, he cautions, "That's me past your image of me" (48). Imagine the man between sand dune and waveline, or on the "red jag of a headland" (72); then look past the man. You'll see the poetry. You'll see the Island he came from. It finds its line and form in his poetry. His landscapes were never merely topography. They were written inward on brain and heart. His intimate relationship with Island landscapes shaped his perceptual and linguistic habits. His language contains hills and coves, the "red gouges of creeks" (103), and a limitless North Shore horizon.

With economy and deftness, Acorn re-creates Island landscapes, and he reflects upon Island community, particularly upon the farmers, fishers, and dockers, who composed so much of the community as it was in his day. Attentive in his strong-lined portraits to the "fissured" hands of

---

[2] Hereinafter referred to as *Selected Poems*.

labourers, the "gutted cheeks" of dockers (49), Acorn draws Island people, as he does its landscape, with a delicate facility that complements his tough realism. Because of his fine acuity of eye and ear, Acorn challenges the Island visitor, as well as the native-born, to an acute noticing, and he recalls to the reader what it is he or she has carelessly passed by without regard. His poems command the reader to "Look up," look at, listen. Not only does Acorn's poetry make visible and audible an Island world, but also his poetry is an entrance to Island language. The "lilt and cut" (103) of the Island voice is heard in Acorn's poetry. By concentrating the best of Acorn's Island verse in one volume, *The Edge of Home* highlights the uniqueness of his perceptions, the appropriateness of his language.

Arranged chronologically, *The Edge of Home* unfolds Acorn's poetic journey through Island meadows and fields, communities and work places. Poems have been selected from Acorn's successive volumes, but, in each case, the last published version of the poem has been chosen. The selection reflects his formal development as well as the evolution of his vision of the Island. Stylistically, Acorn begins with received forms (the quatrain chiefly) in the self-published *In Love and Anger* (1956); adopts an Imagistic economy and precision for the depiction of landscape and its inhabitants (poems that appear in the volumes of 1960, 1963, and 1969); employs the longer, looser line for the political and historical material of *More Poems for People* (1972) and *The Island Means Minago* (1975),[3] and concludes with the sonnet.

The trajectory traced in his formal development corresponds with shifts in focus. Up until 1975, his attention, when writing about Island subjects, is upon landscape and its inhabitants. In *Minago*, this attention is combined with Island history and politics, and, in his final sonnet-writing period, as represented by *Captain Neal MacDougal* (1982), Acorn moves into the realm of myth, articulating, as he says, a "strange spirituality" (*Captain Neal* 12). His development, in short, is from the realism of the early Imagist work to the mythic vision of *Captain Neal*. The arrangement of these poems follows Acorn from land to sea, from realism to myth. There is, of course, continuity as well as change in Acorn's "travels" through Island materials: a tone, compassionate and combative, prevails.

---

[3] Hereinafter referred to as *Minago*.

Moreover, even in the early Imagist landscapes, there is a remarkable fascination with the sea: many of those poems position the speaker, or a protagonist, on the shore. In *Captain Neal*, through his protagonist, Acorn embarks upon the sea that was for so long the focus of his gaze.

From the very first book, but particularly in the 1970s — when he was associated with the Canadian Liberation Movement and published by NC Press — Acorn was, of course, a political polemicist in verse, but even in his most politically strident volume, *More Poems for People* (1972), he places, at about the middle of the volume, a poem like "The Sea." It is as if Acorn in the midst of his wide-ranging political preoccupations recalls the sound and significance of his sea-surrounded origins. Just as he made frequent return visits to the Island during his years away, so also his poetry — even when it ranged widely in subject — never entirely lost touch with its generative source. As a result, this selection of his Island pieces includes Acorn at all stages of his career: the poet life-long. From the "edge of home," a phenomenological as well as a physical place for Acorn, he discoursed loudly on the world and its troubles; he wrote and ranted. The poet of wide-ranging politics is not an *invention* (to use his term) disconnected from the poet of Island meadows.

Although the chief purpose of the edition is to gather the Milton Acorn Island story into one volume, the incidental aesthetic gain is that the best of Acorn appears here. His finest poems — there is significant critical agreement on this — are concerned with the Island. The passionate politics of *The Island Means Minago*, for example, is free of the preachiness that besets his other political work. An imaginative rather than a strictly historical retelling of a nineteenth-century Island feud, *Minago* is politics enriched with wit and humour.

2

Acorn's Island is not often an idyllic haven. He records its weather of tranquility and storm; its periods of peace and war; the wretchedness, as well as the contentment, of its inhabitants. If the Island is, as he says, "a visible sample of heaven" (*Minago* 98), it has also been — upon his telling — a zone of conflict. In *The Island Means Minago*, he gives imaginative shape to the century-long conflict between tenants and absentee landlords that preceded Confederation, and he links the earlier struggle to present-day conditions. Off-Island ownership of valuable lands, particularly Island shoreline, is a reversion, according to Acorn, to a previous condition: *"The landlords are coming back..."* (*Minago* 80). The feisty tone of *Minago* is a continuation, not a correction, of his earlier Island work. In the volumes before *Minago*, Acorn depicted Islanders' struggle with the elements, and, in his portraits of people (carpenters, seamen, rural women), he focused upon the economic and social struggle of workers for security and dignity. But *Minago*, with its depth of history, makes political conflict a principal subject. It might be supposed that Acorn's years away, in Montreal, Toronto, and Vancouver, account for · the politicization of his Island materials. Such an interpretation would ignore, however, the presence, from the beginning, in his Island poetry of the motif of strife. He did, after all, describe his poetry as "pale *bayonets* of grass waving thin on dunes" (italics added; 68).

A realist in his depiction of place and people, Acorn nonetheless believed his Island a scrap of heaven, one worth fighting for. Geophysical circumstance — the surrounding (sometimes savage) sea and wicked weather conditions — were the nursery of the warrior mentality. His pastoralism is a claim asserted, a vision held to, in the face of conditions "grim...black and cold," as the first poem in this volume describes them. *"[T]he dreamlike Island landscape"* (*Minago* 64) that prevails in three seasons of the year disappears in winter, particularly towards its end in "the last stormtime" when the "living" scarcely "remember" who they are, and the groan of trees and the "hiss of the snows" seem to be "the ghosts of ancestors...wandering," as baffled and confused in the "stormtime" as the living are (86). Moreover, the achieved "Pastoral" view of the Island, in the first and last verses of the poem of that name, brackets social truths that are far from Edenic. The eye that carefully discriminates differences in the flight patterns of gull and tern does not avert its glance from the sea's "bullets of spray" (59) or from the stain of blood on Island earth. Pastoral his home may be by times, but the Island is also the Blakean forge of his personal anger, as it is in his most famous poem, "I've Tasted My Blood."

This selection of Acorn's poems includes pieces explicitly about the Island or Islanders and poems on other subjects that take the Island as a reference point. In *The Edge of Home*, the reader will find Island history and Island places, from Great George Street (Charlottetown) to the North Shore. These poems contain images of ploughed fields and pastures; trout ponds and rivers "tunnel[ing] under the elms" (53); the shore and sea, including the sailboats of the present, the schooners of the past. The "business of wind" (64) — its calm and squall — is of interest to Acorn, as are the moods of the ocean. The avian poems, as well as some of the rural poems ("Images for the Season" 56), are indeterminate as to setting, but the bird-watcher was Island-bred. The several carpenter poems may or may not be based on Acorn's years as an Island carpenter, but at least one of these (66), according to biographer Richard Lemm, is a portrait of an uncle with whom Acorn worked. There are poems such as "Mike," "Belle," and "Those Country Guys" (48, 52, 113) that draw attention to speech habits, including the poet's own. How a person pronounces his or her own name, Acorn believed, geographically places that person. When Acorn writes portrait poems such as these, whether or not the person is an Islander, the poem pivots on Acorn's notation of a speech habit different from, or similar to, his own: "I'm geared different, Mike, to a nod / and look over wavy water, my name / pronounced with a rolling tongue…" (48). There are poems here about Acorn family members, present and past generations, and poems such as "Pastoral" (65) and "Picasso's Seated Acrobat with Child" (47) about "[t]he child I growing" (47) that say something about the poet's childhood mind.

Arguably, Acorn's love poems do not belong here unless, as in the case of "Live With Me on Earth" (81), the dwelling to which the beloved is invited is the "leafy…little spaces" and "spruce copse" (81) so familiar in his other Island poems. Admittedly, Acorn sometimes conflates places as he does in "Live With Me on Earth": the "bluebirds" in that poem have flown in from another landscape, a mythical one perhaps. Even when a poem's setting is indeterminate, as in "Knowing I Live in a Dark Age" (68), where the period not the place is of importance, signal Island features — "grass waving thin on dunes" — crop up. His poems carried the Island landscape with them wherever he went; for this reason, the collection is subtitled "Milton Acorn from the Island." In poems undefined as to setting, it is the casual unselfconscious intrusion of a home image that pulls the poem back to this shore. Not as a geographer, but as a descendant-poet of the Island, the editor looked for the familiar Island sights, sounds, and habits in Acorn's work.

Included as well are poems on the "craft of poetry" because Acorn's poetics are inextricably bound up with the intricacies of Island landscape; the relationship of "craft" and landscape is the subject of the interpretive essay that follows. The essay argues that Acorn's prosodic conceptions and development were intimately connected to his responses to Island landscape and character. *The Edge of Home* includes poems that speak in a self-aware manner about the origins, nature, and unfolding of the poetic process. The introductory essay — in its concern with place and poetics — makes reference to these autobiographical poems on poetics. The Introduction is one Islander's understanding of what Acorn wrote about her place, her people; one reader's engagement with the poetics of the Island's pre-eminent poet.

Works Cited

Acorn, Milton. *Captain Neal MacDougal and the Naked Goddess: A Demi-Prophetic Work as a Sonnet-Series.* Charlottetown: Ragweed, 1982.

——. *Dig Up My Heart: Selected Poems 1952-83.* Toronto: McClelland and Stewart, 1983, 1994.

——. *The Island Means Minago.* Toronto: NC Press, 1975.

Deahl, James. Introduction. *The Uncollected Acorn.* Toronto: Deneau, 1987

Lemm, Richard. *Milton Acorn: In Love and Anger.* Ottawa: Carleton UP, 1999.

The Ecological Poetics of Milton Acorn's Island Poems[1]

Edges are wild, sometimes unpredictable places....
— Kate MacQuarrie, *Life at the Edge*

In the three books that followed the self-published "In Love and Anger" (1956), Milton Acorn discovered a poetic form appropriate to the "beloved reality" of his home (106).[2] Contrary to Michael Ondaatje's claim that Canada "is really not the country" for Imagism since the form is inadequate to "the vastness of our place [and] our vast unspoken history" (11), Acorn finds Imagism suitable to his part of the country — the crescent island in the Gulf of St. Lawrence. In Acorn's work of the 1960s — *The Brain's the Target* (1960), *Jawbreakers* (1963), and *I've Tasted My Blood* (1969) — Canadian poetry makes "a return to Imagism" (33), Dorothy Livesay observes. Acorn's early Imagistic Island poetry rises naturally from a landscape "plotted and pieced" (to use Hopkins' phrase [68]), a landscape intricately and minutely patterned. Acorn responded to the small-scale physical economy of the Island with the small-scale Imagist poem. "To be born on an island's to be sure / You are native with a habitat" (92), Acorn pronounced in words that anticipate D. M. R. Bentley's critical work *The Gay] Grey Moose*, a theory of ecological poetics. In their technical and formal aspects, Bentley argues, poems manifest an "equivalence" with the spatial features of the external world of which they are an "integral and inescapable part..." (10).

In "The Island," the defining poem of the 1960 volume, *The Brain's the Target*, Acorn's Imagistic precision is directly and self-referentially

---

[1] The ideas presented here were first introduced in "Milton Acorn's PEI Poems: An Ecological Approach" at *Message in a Bottle: The Literature of Small Islands* International Conference and Literary Festival, 24–28 June 1998, in Charlottetown. The argument was further developed in "Milton Acorn's Poetry: The Biography of an Island" in *Telling Lives*, Institute of Island Studies 18th Annual Island Lecture series, 17 April 2000, in Charlottetown; and in "Realism and Pastoralism: Milton Acorn's Prince Edward Island Poems" at *Islands: Dream and Reality* International Conference, 29 June–1 July 2000, Centre for Manx Studies, Douglas, Isle of Man.
[2] Quotations of poems that appear in *The Edge of Home* are indicated by page reference only. When the author quotes poems that do not appear in this volume, the page numbers refer to *Dig Up My Heart: Selected Poems 1952–83* (abbreviated as *Selected* in the parenthetical bracket) or to poems in other collections by Acorn. All titles are abbreviated in the parenthetical brackets.

linked to Island landscape: "Since I'm Island-born home's as precise /
as if a mumbly old carpenter, /... laid it out, / refigured to the last three-
eighths of shingle" (53). The precision of home demands an exactitude
in language. Formal features of Acorn's early poetry — his minimalism,
his preference for the concrete over the abstract, and his precision of
detail — reflect upon his place of origin. Words in poetry, he said in an
interview, should be those used "in ordinary conversation, in the locality
where you were brought up" (Pearce 99). Just as he prescribes a socially
exact language, so also he was always striving for an ecologically exact
form and language. "[W]here you were brought up" will render some
poetic forms more favourable than others. Like the flora and fauna he
writes about, Acorn's poems are integral with the "habitat."

An island, however, is not only its landscape; it is also the sea that
surrounds it. Vastness — oceanic expanse — is part of an islander's
consciousness. An island poetry will reflect the double rhythm of
local "habitat" and vastness, accommodate, that is, the contrary spatial
experiences of bounded space and boundlessness. In Acorn's *oeuvre*,
spatial vastness and the vastness of history, which Ondaatje believes
are best accommodated in the long poem, find their suitable form in
the flexible sonnet, his "Jackpine sonnet," which, according to Acorn,
grows at opportunity, responding to circumstance (*Jackpine Sonnets* 24).
The seamanship that Acorn prescribes in his poem "The Squall" aptly
describes his deft manipulation of a traditional "craft," the flexibility he
brought to the received form of the sonnet:

> When you're caught in an eight-foot boat — seaworthy
> though —
> You've got to turn your back, for a man rows backwards
> Taking direction from the sting of rain and spray.
> How odd, when you think of it, that a man rows backwards!
> ....
>
> It'll do no good if you head straight to sea.
> You've got to make a nice calculation
> Of where you're going, where you want to be,
> What you need, and possibility;
> ....   (97–98)

Acorn's variations on the sonnet — as to the number of lines, line lengths, and rhyme scheme — discover "[w]hat you need, and possibility," as called for by the demands of subject. The best use to which he put his sonnet was his last collection, *Captain Neal MacDougal & the Naked Goddess* (1982). Oceanic vastness and the vastness of history are both present. Whereas the poems of the early period — poems about Island landscapes and the people of those landscapes — practise an Imagist economy, in his late poems, he adopts the variable sonnet for panoramas, which, by the 1980s, had become predominantly seascapes, or poems concerned with seafaring men. In Imagism and sonnet, and in the techniques that accompanied those forms, Acorn crafted a poetry ecologically suited to his subjects: Island landscapes and seascapes respectively. His early Imagist work and his *Captain Neal* sonnets share a virtuosity of language and form that was not always present in his middle polemical period as, for example, in the 1972 *More Poems for People*. Moreover, these two forms, the Imagist poem and the sonnet (first featured in the 1977 *Jackpine Sonnets*), are connected by the dialectical method, which originated in the early Island landscapes, and which he trumpeted in the introduction to the *Jackpine Sonnets*, where he made it the principle of the form. The dialectical method, this essay will argue, owes more to Acorn's early experience of the Island than it does to politics. Although the Petrarchan sonnet is inherently dialectical in working out its argument (octave and sestet), Acorn, even before he employed it, saw landscapes, objects, and persons in dialectical terms.

In between these two forms, Imagism and sonnet, and sometimes overlapping them, Acorn's poetry — often rambunctious political material — flowed into longer, more discursive lines, marked, occasionally, by strange punctuation and typographical experimentation. "I was playing games through most of this whole Vancouver period," he told interviewer Jon Pearce (99). In too many of the political poems, imagery disappears in exhortation; public prescription replaces personal perception. In those political poems that do succeed, what convinces, Ed Jewenski observes (and he is half-right), is "not theory or political thought, but an unhesitating sense of lyricism, point of view, imagery, and rhythmic subtlety" (36), a finesse honed on Island landscapes.

Acorn's "political thought" in regards to the Island is not, however, so easily separable from the rhythm of his speech or his "point of view," as Jewenski suggests.

Most scholars recognize that Acorn's poetry of place is superior to his polemics, but while preferring the former, they sometimes register a grievance about his regionalism. Reviewing *The Brain's the Target* (1960), Milton Wilson notes, regretfully, that "the Maritime regionalist (admirable in himself) is allowed to overshadow the debater, and Mr. Acorn's development seems truncated" ("Letters," 1961, 395), and even Michael Gnarowski, with his clear preference for Acorn's poetry of place and portraits of people, is apologetic: "Acorn proves that while his orientation may be frequently regional, the clean and strong poetry which he shapes out of sharp impressions can range very capably well beyond his favourite 'Island'" (124). Capability is proven, apparently, only in the extra-regional reach. Although George Bowering notices that it is in the "imagist poem... [Acorn] achieves his most accomplished acts" (94), Bowering fails to link this accomplishment to Island geography. Typically, the reviewers of Acorn's early volumes acknowledged Acorn's Imagist poems with a parenthetically dismissive gesture — "(some of his best poems are brief imagistic pieces)" — divorcing his Imagism from his "serious" work and, worse, construing it as uniformly "quiet" (Wilson, "Letters," 1964, 375–76). Examination of Acorn's early poems reveals a close connection between the poet's perceptual habits, on the one hand, and the place that he writes about, on the other. It further reveals that his language habits are integral to the dialectic that he discerned, from the beginning, in Island life and nature.

1

The minutiae of Island landscapes, of which he was passionately conscious, importuned the Imagist. Acorn was so permeable to the sights and sounds of his place, he was, in effect, the province of their expression: he translated the elements and physical attributes of place into language. Lyric joy accompanies the dazzle of discernment, the acuity of eye and ear, in his work. As Livesay notes, "lyricism inevitably canters alongside" Imagism in Acorn's poetry of the 1960s (33).

The congruity of perception and language communicates the pleasure that eye, brain, and tongue discover in conveying the momentary way of things. Eye, brain, and tongue — this is the physiology Acorn frequently refers to in his poetry. Eye and tongue correspond to perception and language, but the brain was the means by which the beauty outside became "the beauty inside me" (65). For Acorn, the brain was the target of physical sensation. Acorn's early poetry is a record not of things, but of the apprehension of the sensation of things. The sensorium — the supposed seat of sensation in the brain — is, according to Acorn, an impressionable waterside. "[A]nd the waters / of my brain shake" is his response to powerful experience (69). He depicted mental landscapes in terms of the physical landscapes — watery and wind-riven — familiar to him.

In Acorn's poetry, there is a cartography of the brain as well as of the landscape. In "Encounter," he describes a carpenter's shift of attention from his "sawcut" to the figure (the speaker) standing before him:

he lets each word,
slant of your chin,
each eyelid flicker
drip from level to level

in his brain
and be counted…
trying to fit you too
into his pictures.

(60)

Acorn imagined the brain, the brain's work, as it took in information, figured and fit it "into… pictures." His poetry reveals how phenomena present themselves in the mind. Like his "One-Eyed Seaman," Acorn was a "sceptic believing in a strong pulse" — sensation's record (*Selected* 24). Because of his constant attention to "'Inwardness, / outwardness… And the going to and fro between them'" (*Tasted* 114), his theory of poetry and his poetic practice are inseparable from the Island landscapes to which he paid such close attention.

Acorn's poetic was driven by a need to describe the world around him:

"you've got to represent it," he said, "in concrete terms… as a rule I begin with something concrete, something sensory… my intention [is] to get the *exact impression*" (italics added; Pearce 94, 97). Acorn's use of the word "impression" signals his awareness of the transience in his "beloved reality." The apprehension of such a moment (the fleeting "impression") is, however, inscribed with the personality of the observer. As he said in an interview, what matters is "the way you sign your subject — by the use of the hard, precise description" (Pearce 98). It is that "hard, precise description," as well as the economy of description, that makes his poetry Imagistic, and makes it, at the same time, distinctively his own. Imagist poetry is, according to John T. Gage, inevitably subjective (130).

In Acorn's work, there is tremendous pressure around the moment: "sudden time" (65) is the temporal dimension of apprehension. However "hard [and] precise" the resulting description, the occasion of discernment was for Acorn a transcendent moment of intense sensory awareness. In a moment of "inlet vision," as he describes it in the poem "Perfect," he is crossed by the light, "a slit of light, / blinding, sudden" (*Selected* 127–28). Believing in, and living for, those transcendent sensory moments, Acorn was no less a realist. He knew such moments were won in paying patient attention to the transient.

The call in an Acorn poem is "Look up" (71), look at; he commands attention to sudden shifts in the visual world: "'Look up!' / at three geese scooting low'" (71). Those commended in an Acorn poem are people of visual acuity, like the foreman in "House" who "scan[s] earth / at his feet / as if the house / stood there, / him figuring, / edging, / adjusting" (71). "Charlottetown Harbour" is about a spell of "glinting" light that claims the attention of an old docker.

In "Poem," composed in 1960, and revised in 1975, he says, "My soul's no white wind-balanced gull," but a "hunchback dangerous snuffling thing / whose salvation's *the taste of the moment*" (italics added; 115). His aptitude for the moment enabled him to grasp what exists in the "blink":

> One day in a lifetime
> I saw one with wings
> a pipesmoke blur

Milton Acorn

shaped like half a kiss
and its raspberry-stone
heart winked fast in
a thumbnail of a breast.

In that blink it
was around a briar
and out of sight, but
I caught a flash
of its brain
where flowers swing
udders of sweet cider;
....

("Hummingbird" 46)

Not only sights but sounds are tensely attended to. He practised a disciplined listening: "Hear with the wind still, the grass still, / sharp and erect like animal ears, / its green darkened, / the air and its light dark green // birds hidden in the just trembling / leaves… [and] the rustle of the rain coming on" (79). The reader is enjoined to hear with stillness. Auditory perceptions sharpen sight so that the green of the grass is found to be "darkened" by stillness, "the air and its light" rendered "dark green." The poem is a record of a precise moment — "the just trembling / [of] leaves," the just-so of things. In Acorn's poetry, the Island is a space acutely listened to as in "the trickle of water / from raised oars" in "The Trout Pond" (54), or the "brook truckling thru log-breaks and cedars" in the 1963 "Pastoral" (65).

Acorn's attunement to sudden shifts in visual and auditory phenomena, combined with his language dexterity, enabled him to communicate with images, which is the primary feature of Imagist poetry. Real communication between human beings, T. E. Hulme theorized in the early twentieth century, occurs by way of images (Pratt 27). Acorn's poised and quiet attendance upon things intuited their complex relations: "I'd like to mark myself / quiet" — "something // like a tree in winter" that "bears its lines and clusters / of snow, as if what's fallen / on it were its own" (75). Not only does he long for tree's quietude, but also he is perceptive about the "intricate jointure" of tree and snow. The intricacy of a thing — whether it is the "intricate jointure" of a living body (69) or the "intricate" construction of a schooner (74) — or the complex relations among things is often the object of his focus. "Which is the sun and which is the wind / Sweeping like a yellow broom?" is the rhetorical question that he frames in "Apple Tree in the Wind" (85).

Perceptions — whether of the snow-covered tree or the apple tree — are brought home to the domestic: "The stove is waiting and humming" for the fruit of the tree, which will be made "[i]nto applesauce… by my mother" (85). The localization of perception in the domestic is a function of an eye that is rooted in the heart (*Selected* 71). The eye is never optical only, never heart-less. Nevertheless, the "optic heart" (to use Margaret Avison's phrase [17]) must be "stronghearted" enough to look at the real, or to be "realisant" ("Introduction," *Jackpine Sonnets* 24): "If you're stronghearted look at this Island; / red gouges of creeks at low tide and / the stronger red which spreads behind plows" (103). Acorn's rigorous precision comprehends the clash of forces that results in "red gouges."

The Imagist focused upon the intricate order of landscape and its objects is also aware of order's opposite, anarchy, the way in which the "intricate tension of atoms" (47) can explode into chaos. The polarity — intricacy and anarchy — which can be traced throughout the entire *oeuvre*, is first found in the early Island landscapes. Listening to and looking at his "sweeping," "humming" world, Acorn registered the anarchic energy that lies just the other side of the "intricate" orderliness of the Island pastoral.

2

Committed to an "exact impression" of his dynamic domestic world, Acorn's early poems are often a notation of contrasts: past and present, action and stasis, land and sea exist in oppositional tension. Dialectics, as Acorn defined it, is "'the philosophy of contradictions'" (Barker 161). The "artist's knack of looking squarely at contradictions and allowing them to work themselves out in his poems" carries the dialectic into the poem ("Open Letter" 288). In whatever way Acorn might have used, or misused, the term politically (Gudgeon 20, 65–66), in this instance, "dialectics" refers to a poetic principle, one that he had encountered in his reading of Dylan Thomas, who wrote, "an image must be born and die in another; and any sequence of my images must be a sequence of creations, recreations, destructions, contradictions" (qtd. in Treece 37). Thomas referred to this as his "dialectical method" (37). Acorn's "Open Letter to a Demi-Senior Poet" begins "Dear Dylan" (287). A dialectical movement between contraries is present in Acorn's earliest landscapes and in the portraits of the people of those landscapes. His language practices (minimalism and concreteness) ensure a tense opposition among things: this is a poetry composed largely of nouns, and his nouns are monosyllables, craggy and charged with energy.

Even in poems such as "Retired Carpenter," "Hands," and "Inland Gull," where a single object is the focus of attention, the dialectical movement between opposites is perceptible. In the first verse of "Retired Carpenter,"

> Tools, grips sweat-polished,
> in a dinted box, loose
> at all angles,
> half of them vanished [,]

(66)

the object (existing in terms of glisten, contour, and angle) is presented abruptly and economically, without articles, without conjunctions, a practice that Acorn believed paralleled daily speech: people "speak in short, clipped sentences, designed to communicate information quickly... drop[ping] almost all articles and conjunctions" (*Hundred Proof Earth* 56). In spite of its brevity and single-image focus, the poem manages to contrast Old Stan's retirement (of the second verse) with a labour-intense past, which has resulted in the "sweat-polished" tools and the dented tool-box. The metonymy glimpses at the worker Stan once was, and no longer is. Similarly, the poem given over to a description of "Hands" that are "dyed / earth and tobacco brown" conveys toughness and delicacy at once in "a grip all courtesy" (67), but it is in the single-image landscape poem that the practice of contraries is most evident. "Inland Gull" contrasts the bird's whiteness to "a dirty woollen sky," where the scriptorial gull "scratches arrogance on brittle gusts" (78). Avian defiance is subtly aligned with writing.

Acorn scaled the world down to objects — objects in conflict, or objects embedded in contrary states. His images are dense and concrete. He further concretized descriptive imagery through his noun-compounded adjective. The "land-buffed" air of "Inland Gull" is typical of the language economy of his descriptive imagery, which, according to Acorn, is "the most effective of poetic devices [surpassing metaphor and conceit]... . compelling a poet to probe deeply into the reality of phenomenon..." (*Hundred Proof Earth* 55). Interestingly, he finds Yeats's "'That dolphin-torn, that gong-tormented sea,'" (55) to be an exemplary descriptive line without noticing its similarity to his own habit of the hyphenated adjective, as in "Old Property": "Past the *frost-cracked* rock step / twist yourself thru / skewgee trunks and old *coat-hook* branches..." (italics added; 50). Acorn is an adjectival Imagist, and the adjective does double duty. A noun substantiates the adjectival phrase; the modifier attributes tension to the modified noun. Nowhere is this more obvious than when he describes himself as "Island-born":

> Since I'm Island-born home's as precise
> as if a mumbly old carpenter,
> shoulder-straps crossed wrong,
> laid it out,
> refigured to the last three-eighths of shingle.
>
> Nowhere that plough-cut worms
> heal themselves in red loam;
> spruces squat, skirts in sand;
> or the stones of a river rattle its dark
> tunnel under the elms,
> is there a spot not measured by hands;
> no direction I couldn't walk
> to the wave-lined edge of home.
> ...

(53)

Deploring the adjective, the Anglo-American Imagists, as a rule, stuck to nouns, but Acorn gives to the adjective the concreteness of the noun. Not only is there density and pent-up energy in this practice, but also his adjectival form of Imagism pre-empts simplicity with wit. The violence of "plough-cut worms" toughens the potentially sentimental image of the healing powers of red earth and balances the domestic metaphor "spruces squat, skirts in sand," itself a trope of great economy. Wit is similarly present in the doubly meant "shingle" (line 5), which looks forward to the beach-shingle on the "wave-lined edge" of the Island (line 13). Acorn told an interviewer, "if you can incorporate the reminiscences of a noun into an adjective, it's all the better. Again and again the poem must have words that bring images with them" (Pearce 98).

"Nowhere" on this domesticated Island, Acorn explains, "is there a spot not measured by hands." Everywhere his Island landscapes bear reminiscences of the lives lived there, the labour accomplished, as, for example, in the frequent references to hands. The old docker at "Charlottetown Harbour" has "used-up-knuckled hands" (49), and the hands of the farmer are "fissured" with labour (67). The past is dialectically positioned in relation to the present. The wear on the hands of these workers inscribes a past that is the antithesis of their retirement. The time-arrested docker, mesmerized by "a spell of the glinting water," is contrasted with a younger self belonging to a past of dynamic movement, when life was brave and "masts stood up like stubble" (49). The stasis of the present is contrasted with an organic past of productive action. Acorn's labourers represent an Island economic and social past that has given way to a crumbling present: "waves slop among the weed-grown piles" in "Charlottetown Harbour" (49).

If "[p]oetry demands an exactitude / That defies description" (*Selected* 93), then language must create the presence, not just the look, of an object, and this is especially urgent when the poem's focus is the clash of elements in Island weather. A person exposed to those elements is pummelled in the clash. "Lee Side In a Gale," through word choice, hyphenated adjective, and organization, enacts the maul of the gale. Beginning offshore, at sea's horizon, the gale, like the poem, gathers force, as it worries out the speaker's hiding place to deliver an "all-of-a-sudden" whack (73). Even in the opening visual presentation of the distant skyline, the jerky effect of "a jumpity-jagged, beat-up / mercury saw of a skyline" is evidence of the gale's moving on the sea. Gerund adjectives, rather than his usual noun compound, create the action on the horizon, and the "[b]lack" of the sea indicates its temper, rather than its colour. This word choice, as Acorn explains it, is consistent with the way the "people of Prince Edward Island would use the words 'dark' and 'black' interchangeably" (Pearce 97). "Lee Side" installs some of Acorn's best technical effects, and combines them with the "startling" moment to which he was so attuned.

The quick-work effects of elements, and the fierce mechanisms of nature, require the brevity of Imagism, not the duration of the long poem. Acorn's superb deployment of the Imagist line is obvious in his hinged (at "and") poem "Nature" (62). The swift delivery of images in this poem reinforces a cruel irony. The automatic response of "nestlings" to coolness betrays them into mistaking a cat's murderous intentions for maternity. Line and language — concrete, noun-dense, and explosive — render a world rife with oppositions.

From the outset, Acorn's Island poems incorporated the war of forces inherent in nature; an oppositional relation between past and present; and, most importantly, the tension between bounded space and boundless sea, which is the very definition of an Island. After careful attention in the first two verses of "The Island" (above quoted) to the measured, calculated, bounded space of its landscape, Acorn, in the third and last verse, turns to the "fanged jaws of the Gulf" within which the Island lies. If Island space is figured and "refigured to the last three-eighths of shingle," its plotted and pieced certainties end at the "wave-lined edge…" (53). The double, and contradictory, features of Island space are measure and edge. Past that edge is the sea, a perilous shape-shifter. The antithesis of greatest importance in Acorn's early poetry is that of land and sea, the known and the unknown. The known is comfortingly familiar, intricately patterned; the unknown is anarchic.

In "November Beach," published three years after "The Island," Acorn contrasts shore and water as "stone frozen rippled sand" and "ocean tumbling from the skyline" (59). As is usual in the early Imagistic landscapes, the speaker is positioned on land glancing outward. His gaze is challenged: "The water of your eye freezes." Only the ducks, further out, dare movement: "zig-zagging / amidst the bullets of spray" (59). The ocean is a zone of danger; only the hardy, using guerrilla manoeuvres, venture there. In the early Imagist work, the poet remains on shore, gazing outward.

3

The hardihood of ancestral Islanders is Acorn's subject in *The Island Means Minago* (1975), a volume that imaginatively dramatizes nineteenth-century Island history. In their struggle against the agents of absentee landlords, the tenants vow to "keep [their] thoughts strong / As lead and powder…" (*Minago* 19) while, at the same time, deploying a "twisty, riddley" speech intended to confuse rent collectors, the landlords' agents. The ancestors' strategy includes intellectual and verbal resistance as well as physical. In the essay, "Islanders are…," included in the volume, Acorn deconstructs clichés that represent Islanders as "the slow-moving, slow-thinking, kindly products of a land where history has marked time for centuries" (*Minago* 95).

In *Minago*, as in the verse drama *The Road to Charlottetown* (1998), with which it shares the nineteenth-century story, the Islanders' gait is a calculated tactic of deception in their engagement with British forces. The verbal and physical characteristics that are often derisively ascribed to Islanders are, thereby, claimed and politicized. In *Minago*, Island history is exclusively conflictual, and history — like "habitat" in the earlier volumes — shapes character.

Even Island landscape, according to Acorn, can be read politically. In "The Figure in the Landscape Made the Landscape," the Island's physical features are the result of a war strategy. The figure in the landscape (in an "imagined / Pre-Confederation" painting) and his fellow-revolutionaries of the period are the architects of the Island's pattern of "Clearings and woodlots, clearings and woodlots" since the woodlot was, supposedly, a tactic in a guerrilla war with land agents, and bending roads were "laid out for war" (102). Present-day tourists are the "gulls" of this far-off joke since they see the effect (landscape pattern), but are ignorant of the cause. Moreover, these tourists are "pawns" in a "new still-just-brooding / Struggle for the land." In the *Minago* essay "Islanders are…," Acorn approaches this subject humourously: "Once a bunch of Sports came over and organized Confederation.... Those Sports kept coming, more and more. We didn't object because The Island is a visible sample of Heaven," but now that tourism is an "industry," "so many Sports come here in summertime it's hard to find an Islander in all that crowd" (*Minago* 98). Elsewhere in *Minago*, he refers to the industry's selling of the Island way of life — "'Holiday Island' and 'The Million Acre Playground'" — as a *"savage racket"* (*Minago* 64).

In "I, Milton Acorn," part self-portrait, part legal declamation, Acorn aligns himself with ancestors; his fight for his "opinion[s]" with the tenants' war on landlords: "The Island's small... Every opinion counts / I'm accustomed to fighting for them" (92). With the ancestors, he shares "a tortuous all-odds-counting manner / Of thinking [that] marks me an Islander" (92). Linking the past to the present, Acorn explodes the idea that the Island is, or ever was, a "pocket" of safety in an otherwise troubled world: "Come from an Island to which I've often returned / Looking for peace, and usually found strife." Employing his preferred analogy, one that links weather and warfare, Acorn delights in the present-day strife because "after all my favourite mode / Of weather's been a hurricane." The "strife" to which he refers — permeating the Island as elsewhere — is the "glorious" struggle of the present wherein "the ancient rule of classes is hit / And hit again. History's greatest change / Is happening." According to Acorn's way of thinking, living on an island is superb preparation for the struggle: "Growing up on one's good training...." In *Minago*, Island landscape and climate determine character; and Islanders, in turn, use landscape strategically. A homage to ancestors, and a comparison of contemporary class relations to those of the past, *Minago* presents in book-length form the intricate connection between place and character that he explored earlier in the compact Imagist portrait poems. Given the circumstances — inequalities, past and present — anarchy, he believes, is as certain as a fall hurricane.

As in the earlier poems, so also in *Minago*, which is landbased since its focus is land ownership, Acorn is sometimes impatient with "limits," desirous of the unknown that lies beyond the "edge of home": "I worry / that I can't today go voyaging / Past the limits of limits..." (*Minago* 72). At the close of *Minago*, the dialectic of class, explored through history, gives way to a dialectic of long-standing in his work: land and sea. The strongest poem in the volume, "The Squall," points towards the voyaging and the writing to come.

"The Squall" marks two shifts from the earlier sea poems. The speaker is no longer observing from the shore and, second, the poem is chiefly concerned with adaptability, with survival, in dangerous conditions: "When you're caught in an eight-foot boat... / You've got to turn your back, for a man rows backwards / Taking direction from the sting of rain and spray" (97). Because the sea is a thing "alive / Young-muscled, wanting to toss you in orbit... // You've got to make a nice calculation," find a position of poise between "[f]earfulness" and "fearlessness." The seamanship of "The Squall" is an analogy for the craftsmanship of poetry. Acorn's "craft" of choice for the seaward journey will be the flexible sonnet. What the Imagist poetic was to the landbased poems, the sonnet is to the subject that is of increasing interest to him: the sea.

4

"The Stormbirds," which appears in Acorn's 1977 collection *Jackpine Sonnets*, signals his formal and imaginative departure into storm. The speaker in this poem explicitly identifies himself with the tern, leaving behind "the dull gulls flock[ing] inland" (104). The sea storm is "where the action is... where nothing stays pinned." The stormbird's flight — "[t]acking, slanting against a forty-knot wind" — is the trajectory of a restless mind. Although traditional in length, "Stormbirds" deviates from conventional sonnet rhyme schemes in accordance with the "swirling" tern's "plumb shifts." The sestet identifies the tern, executing its tactical manoeuvres, with "Realisant souls" — "souls solidly / Set in these unsolid worlds and spaces." In the dialectical encounter of mind with "unsolid worlds and spaces," the mind wins rest in restlessness, an "eternal state" of motion: "Simultaneously I return and go." Acorn begins the introduction to *Jackpine Sonnets* ("Tirade by Way of Introduction") by analogically presenting himself in avian terms: "the greying but still dangerous poet of prey wheels his head.... takes off with power and practiced strokes in the direction [towards formal verse] from which the mob fled" in its rush into "scrambled verse" (*Jackpine* 13), which is what he now calls free verse. As George Elliott Clarke says, Acorn's "jack-pine meters /... couldn't be planed to fit pre-fab verse" (Clarke 43). Acorn describes his variable sonnet as "realisant. It has a basic form, yes, but grows to any shape that suits the light, suits the winds, suits itself" (*Jackpine* 24). In other words, it is an organic form, a form responsive to the elements, "growing" in shape from its basic fourteen-line form.

Except for "The Stormbirds," the *Jackpine* volume is, however, polemic divorced from place, or, more accurately, it's all over the place: "The Canadian Bank Loan to Chile" (*Jackpine* 27). The introduction is a rhetorical tirade on poetics; the sonnets themselves, more tirade than technique. When "The Craft of Poetry's the Art of War," poetry is inevitably a casualty. Although *Jackpine* rehearses the enemy list familiar from *More Poems for People* (1972) — bosses, bureaucracy, the state — the poet of *Jackpine* is largely turned inward, obsessed with his own anger. His aim is to "rage cyclonic" (*Jackpine* 35). He describes "chunks of fury / Rattling about" in the "brain pan" (*Jackpine* 76) much as he had, on other occasions, from the shore, described actual chunks of ice churning in a winter sea. Although *Jackpine* showcases the poetic form that Acorn now prefers, his attention, in sonnets such as "To a Goddam Boss," is focused on the past: with noisy bravado, he recollects "How I ripped lyric fragments from the devil's bloody tongue" (*Jackpine* 34). Acorn is aware of the emptiness of this. "I'm frigged," he says, "no note to play… / Short of getting up and making rage my lord… / Sleepless in Toronto — home of the homesick" (*Jackpine* 38). In *Jackpine*, Acorn is psychologically and poetically stalled.

Despite the backward-looking bluster that predominates, the poet of *Jackpine* does, however, also look forward — toward an engagement of a different sort. Death, the bride, is summoned in the final sonnet, "Invocation." Engagement shifts from the political to the cosmological, towards the "unsolid worlds and spaces" of "The Stormbirds." The poet is reformulating his poetic and himself, making himself available to larger experiences, and for Acorn the sea had always represented those larger experiences. It's time for him to go home, or, at least, back to the place from which the journey can begin. When he writes, in *Jackpine*, of the Island, incalculabilities — unanswerable questions — replace the earlier certainty that came from every "spot…measured": "Who has named these colours…? / Given to this pasture, that oatfield, those slight / Poplars…?" (105). Departure by way of the "wave-lined edge," into liminal space, will do that — disturb certainties.

5

> *There is, one knows not what sweet mystery about this sea,*
> *whose gently awful stirrings seem to speak of some hidden soul*
> *beneath... .*
>
> — Herman Melville, *Moby-Dick*

"[T]he world is wild," Acorn pronounces the marine world through which he follows his "ancestor" Captain Neal MacDougal in the sonnet collection of that title (1982), poems that have, he admits, a "strange spirituality" (*Captain Neal* 9, 10, 12). The seafaring Captain is "turn-of-the-century," a period "not so distant from our own time" although "practitioners" of "'contemporaneity'... pretend that all knowledge gained before them is worthless" (*Captain Neal* 11, 9). The sonnet collection has an oceanic wildness — a wild inventiveness in spite of its narrative thread — that is foreign to the measured assurances of the earlier landbased poems. Perhaps the sonnet form anchored Acorn in the sea of myth he had entered upon. "'Why fear to dream... . / Who told you imagination was dangerous?'" (*Captain Neal* 20), the Captain asks his mates as he scuds through the perilous waters of the imagination, where the "Naked Goddess" "[s]een by him alone," licks a tongue "inward through his brain" (108). *Captain Neal MacDougal & the Naked Goddess* is a comic rite of passage upon the liminal space of the ocean, a place of "depths and silences; / Depths and noises" (110). The ship-confined captain is effectively cut off from civilization, away from family and community. He experiences dislocation and confusion, "A Half-troubled Mind" (*Captain Neal* 41). And when he looks in the mirror, he sees not the known self but "Captain Neal MacJanus": "two strangers I nestle / Inside me..." (*Captain Neal* 38). "The liminal phase," Edward Berry writes, "is a period of indeterminate identity, full of ambiguity and paradox...the individual 'wavers between two worlds'" (*Captain Neal* 4). The Captain experiences disorientation.

During his dreams and visions, more importantly, he undergoes an education. His tutor through it all is the "Naked Goddess," who is sometimes transvestite, as well as naked. The liminar, Captain Neal, travels by way of "Revery," "Dreams," "Vision," "Prayer," and "Parable" (modes of knowing named in the sonnet titles). "[I]t's dreaming rearranges the times," the seaman says (*Captain Neal* 20). The familiar and known of the landbased poems has been replaced by the unfamiliar and unknown, the visible by invisible "depths and silences" (110).

In the earlier Imagist poems, Acorn considered the dialectical relationship of bounded space and boundlessness from the shore. In the sonnet collection, through his persona, Acorn places himself in boundless uncertainty. For the exploration of oceanic wildness and the immersion in history (to correct, what he calls, "alienat[ion]" from our "ancestors" [*Captain Neal* 11–12]), he employs not the long poem but the seachanged sonnet.

In the best and final sonnet of the volume, "The Completion of the Fiddle," Acorn presents the axiom that music is incomplete, uncomprehended, unless there is a "motion" that answers to the fiddle's "calls" (111). The Captain, in this last sonnet, invites the "Reality Goddess" to join him in a dance upon "the planks and polish" of the vessel's deck. The figure of the dance is the complement to the sphere's tune, and the sphere — a "round... about a hollow" — is, of course, the celestial sphere as well as the violin's. The dance, which completes the fiddle, expresses an integrative wholeness that combines the measured steps of Islanders with the wilder "motion" upon oceanic space: the "ancestral phantom" dances on a vessel that rides upon the waves. Lyric joy, which for Acorn originated, years before, in the careful notation of the minutiae of Island landscapes, has moved offshore. Moving across the boundary, the "edge," to oceanic vastness, he chooses a poetic form whose history links him to a centuries-long community of practitioners. Through the sonnet, he negotiates time, space, and mystery and, finally, in the last sonnet, celebrates, through the dance, the indivisibility of the known and the unknown as represented by the shifting boundary of sea and land. "'Where,'" he rhetorically asks, "'is the boundary between the sea and the land? It changes twice in more or less twenty-four hours. Does the tide ever stop at the same place?'" (Pearce 101).

If the sea's movement, as signed by the tide mark, is unfixed, incalculable, one's identity within liminal oceanic space is, also, indeterminate. In "The Peoplefish," a poem published posthumously, Acorn resolves the tension between circumscribed known space and uncharted space.

My brother and I swam the cove
then waded
shoulder to shoulder
with cold water lapping
our nipples.
A seal
(wave of flesh and fur
under the waves) swam 'round;
then curved his neck
and pointed head
out of water
at us so close
we saw the wonder in his eyes.

(*Hundred Proof Earth* 29)

The perceiver has become the perceived. In "The Peoplefish," Acorn is at home in the *other's* gaze: seal and sea encircle him. He is beheld by wonder.

In Acorn's final sonnet series, his stand-in, Captain Neal, is similarly accosted by wonder. The "Reality Goddess" rises from "black" sea to give lessons in ways of knowing that partake of the "depths and silences," the shoreless sea, underlying conscious knowledge. Under her tutelage, Acorn's "beloved reality" is without boundaries.

Contra Ondaatje, Acorn found the sonnet, and the sonnet series, to be an appropriate form for vast space and for the searching it invites. Because his disciplined looking at and listening to Island geography were first wed to the precision of Imagism, spatial vastness and its mystery, when he came to them at the close of his career, retained a formality

— the anchoring shape of the sonnet. The flexibility that he brought to that form enabled his final excursion, the seaward one. Acorn shaped his poetic form to suit his environment: Imagism for the "measured" Island landscape and the variable sonnet for shifting seascape — "nothing it's ever been can be repeated":

> Infinity and finitude play loop-the-loop.
> The sea, in every moment of all its ages
> Has been different from anything it's been
> And different from anything it'll ever be.
> Repetition is impossible... .
>
> (89)

Even when he was a continent away from the Island, as he was in Vancouver, even when politics capsized the poetry, as it does in *More Poems for People* and *Jackpine Sonnets*, he was never away. He carried within him the slap of sea on shore: "My lifepulse moves in waves to hit rocks, / Ebb back, replenish, come on for more shocks" (*Jackpine Sonnets* 66). His Island — not always benign, not always beautiful, yet sometimes both — lies in the North Atlantic, remote from tourist brochures. Its pre-eminent poet was a flawed titan who strode its edge, eyes focused on a variety of seacoast creatures, voice raised, sometimes, in a rage the volume of Lear's. And in the end, like Lear, he could think of nothing better than to "take upon's the mystery of things, / As if we were God's spies."

Works Cited

Acorn, Milton. *The Brain's the Target.* Toronto: Ryerson, 1960.
——. *Captain Neal MacDougal & the Naked Goddess: A Demi-Prophetic Work as a Sonnet-Series.* Charlottetown: Ragweed, 1982.
——. *Dig Up My Heart: Selected Poems 1952–83.* Toronto: McCelland and Stewart, 1983, 1994.
——. *I Shout Love and Other Poems.* Ed. James Deahl. Toronto: Aya, 1987.
——. "In Love and Anger." Montreal: privately published, 1956.
——. *The Island Means Minago.* Toronto: NC Press, 1975.
——. *I've Tasted My Blood: Poems 1956 to 1968.* Selected by Al Purdy. Toronto: Ryerson, 1969.

——. *Jawbreakers*. Toronto: Contact Press, 1963.
——. *Hundred Proof Earth*. Ed. James Deahl. Toronto: Aya, 1988.
——. *Jackpine Sonnets*. Toronto: Steel Rail, 1977.
——. *More Poems for People*. Toronto: NC Press, 1972.
——. "Open Letter to a Demi-Senior Poet." *The Making of Modern Poetry in Canada*. Eds. Louis Dudek and Michael Gnarowski. Toronto: Ryerson, 1970. 287–89.
—— and Cedric Smith. *The Road to Charlottetown*. Ed. James Deahl. Hamilton: Unfinished Monument Press, 1998.
Avison, Margaret. *Winter Sun*. Toronto: U of Toronto P, 1960.
Barker, Terry et al. "An Interview with Milton Acorn." *Intrinsic*. 7–8. (Spring 1979): 160–76.
Bentley, D.M.R. *The Gay] Grey Moose: Essays on the ecologies and mythologies of Canadian Poetry, 1690–1990*. Ottawa: U of Ottawa P, 1992.
Berry, Edward. *Shakespeare's Comic Rites*. Cambridge: Cambridge UP, 1984.
Bowering, George. "Poet and Painter." Rev. of *Jawbreakers*, by Milton Acorn. *Canadian Forum*. 43 (July 1963): 94–95.
Clarke, George Elliott. "To Milton Acorn." *Voices: Canadian Writers of African Descent*. Ed. Ayanna Black. Toronto: HarperCollins, 1992. 43.
Gage, John T. *In the Arresting Eye: the Rhetoric of Imagism*. Baton Rouge: Louisiana State UP, 1981.
Gnarowski, Michael. "Milton Acorn: A Review in Retrospect." *Culture* (Quebec) 25 (June 1964): 119–129.
Gudgeon, Chris. *Out of This World: The Natural History of Milton Acorn*. Vancouver: Arsenal Pulp Press, 1996.
Hopkins, Gerard Manley. *The Major Poems*. London: J. M. Dent, 1979. 68.
Jewenski, Ed. "Milton Acorn (1923–1986)." *Canadian Writers and Their Works*. Poetry Series 7. Eds. Robert Lecker, Jack David, and Ellen Quigley. Intro. George Woodcock. Toronto: ECW Press, 1990. 21–74.
Lemm, Richard. *Milton Acorn: In Love and Anger*. Ottawa: Carleton UP, 1999.
Livesay, Dorothy. "Search for a Style: The Poetry of Milton Acorn." *Canadian Literature* 40 (Spring 1969): 33–42.
Ondaatje, Michael. Introduction. *The Long Poem Anthology*. Ed. Michael Ondaatje. Toronto: Coach House Press, 1979. 11–18.
Pearce, Jon. "The Idea of a Poem: An Interview with Milton Acorn." *Canadian Poetry: Studies, Documents, Reviews*. 21 (Fall/Winter 1987): 93–102.
Pratt, William, ed. *The Imagist Poem*. N. Y.: Dutton, 1963.
Treece, Henry. *Dylan Thomas: 'Dog Among the Fairies.'* N. Y.: John de Graff, 1956.
Wilson, Milton. "Letters in Canada: 1960 (Poetry)." *University of Toronto Quarterly*. 30 (July 1961): 380–401.
——. "Letters in Canada: 1963 (Poetry). *University of Toronto Quarterly*. 33 (July 1964): 374–76.

Anne Compton

SELECTED
POEMS

November

The blue-jays squeal: "More rain! More rain!"
The sky's all blotch and stain.
The colours of Earth are melted down
To dark spruce green and dull grass brown.

Black ducks, last week, held parliament
Up-river there.... Gulls came and went.
Now that they're gone, nor'wester blown,
The grim gulls wheel and bob alone.

Nary a leaf has kept its hold.
The thicket's naked, black and cold.
Then zig-zag, like a skating clown,
The first white flake comes down.

Winter Boarders

Smoke and in a blue halo let a poem grow
Of winter and sky blue as laughter
Tinting immaculate snow,
The crows fasting on their pine pulpits
And all the other birds gone, except
On a white tablecloth of snow,
The chickadees, happy and fat as a chuckle.

Hummingbird

One day in a lifetime
I saw one with wings
a pipesmoke blur
shaped like half a kiss
and its raspberry-stone
heart winked fast in
a thumbnail of a breast.

In that blink it
was around a briar
and out of sight, but
I caught a flash
of its brain
where flowers swing
udders of sweet cider;
and we pass as thunderclouds or,
dangers like death, earthquake, and war,
ignored because it's no use worrying....

By him I mean. Responsibility
Against the threat of termination
by war or other things
is given us as by a deity.

Picasso's Seated Acrobat with Child

The child and the old man's eyes
big and wild as a stallion's.
The child I growing, wanting
towards wizardry and competence.

I've dreamt wizards so competent
suns spun side-on to
a nudge from their spare fingertips.

In his brain-pan dreams, the
intricate tension of atoms,
worlds, and him poised
about to dance into them.

Mike

You, Mike, twisting on words as if
they flushed your kidneys with daylight,
your sunset's smoggy green, hot orange,
and shunters scoot throbbing thru
muddled smoke and the noises of iron.

I'm geared different, Mike, to a nod
and look over wavy water, my name
pronounced with a rolling tongue,
the sky like sails in need of washing
sometimes, then splotched blue,
the wind familiar to my shoulders.

That's me past your image of me:
and the figure I see wincing
at sirens and jack-hammer clatter
is only my image of you, and
behind it, feeding it, is you
with your grin showing one eyetooth,
reckoning the works of a man, tracing
the routes of wire or politics, exclaiming
at your own sudden understanding.

Charlottetown Harbour

An old docker with gutted cheeks,
time arrested in the used-up-knuckled hands
crossed on his lap, sits
in a spell of the glinting water.

He dreams of times in the cider sunlight
when masts stood up like stubble;
but now a gull cries, lights,
flounces its wings ornately, folds them,
and the waves slop among the weed-grown piles.

Old Property

Past that frost-cracked rock step
twist yourself thru
skewgee trunks and old coat-hook branches;
ground once dug and thought of and
never intended for those toadstools.

In the shade past the crashed robins' nest,
past that spilt sunlight see,
his grainy grip on
a hatchet keened to a leaf,
a man in murky denims
whispering curses to the weeds.

Islanders

Would you guess from their broad greeting,
witty tuck of eyelids,
how they putt-putt out with lunch-cans
on sea liable to tangle
and dim out the land between two glances?

Tho their dads toed the decks of schooners,
dodging the blustery rush of capes,
and rum-runner uncles used wit-grease
against the shoot-first Yankee cutters,
they wouldn't be the kind to sail their
                    lobster-boats around the world
for anything less than a dollar-ninety an hour.

Belle

Younger Belle was lonely, but now
the men brandish forearms in her kitchen,
shake themselves out with laughter.
Wives, glad they're not at mischief
respect her jet-black mane from a distance

for she'll have no drinking, have no drinking
have no — well perhaps a little one:
but if the measure get more than "some"
it's "Here's your tea. Where do ye want it
down yer throat or over yer head?"

Edwin with his glasses, his pipe
and freckled spare-tipped fingers
she married at twenty-nine — had to
(everybody had to but
                                        the joke is
she made Edwin sign a certificate
or signed one for him …the tales vary).

Edwin is an excellent carpenter
because, they say, he thinks like a board;
but his joy and vocation is moonshining
in which every bubble tells him what's doing.
Says four words in a day
and two of them are "No ma'am."

There's a contest of daughters for the affections
of the youngest, a son
born beside a mare munching clover.
She bore him alone
and he was most reluctant to breathe.
"Kill or cure!" Belle hissed through teeth
whose canines are long and sharp like a wolf's.
What a whack it was: and what a yell!

Anne Compton

The Island

Since I'm Island-born home's as precise
as if a mumbly old carpenter,
shoulder-straps crossed wrong,
laid it out,
refigured to the last three-eighths of shingle.

Nowhere that plough-cut worms
heal themselves in red loam;
spruces squat, skirts in sand;
or the stones of a river rattle its dark
tunnel under the elms,
is there a spot not measured by hands;
no direction I couldn't walk
to the wave-lined edge of home.

In the fanged jaws of the Gulf,
a red tongue.
Indians say a musical God
took up His brush and painted it;
named it, in His own language,
"The Island."

Milton Acorn

The Trout Pond

for R.F. Acorn, 1897–1968

The woods, spruce twisted
into spooky shapes,
echo the trickle of water
from raised oars.

Above the pale ripples
a redwing blackbird fastens,
legs crooked and beak alert,
to a springing reed.

My father's whiteheaded now,
but oars whose tug
used to start my tendons
pull easily these years.

His line curls, his troutfly drops
as if on its own wings,
marks a vee on the mirrored
ragged spruceheads, and
a crane flapping past clouds.

I've Tasted My Blood

If this brain's over-tempered
consider that the fire was want
and the hammers were fists.
I've tasted my blood too much
to love what I was born to.

But my mother's look
was a field of brown oats, soft-bearded;
her voice rain and air rich with lilacs:
and I loved her too much to like
how she dragged her days like a sled over gravel.

Playmates? I remember where their skulls roll!
One died hungry, gnawing grey porch-planks;
one fell, and landed so hard he splashed;
and many and many
come up atom by atom
in the worm-casts of Europe.

My deep prayer a curse.
My deep prayer the promise that this won't be.
My deep prayer my cunning,
my love, my anger,
and often even my forgiveness
that this won't be and be.
I've tasted my blood too much
to abide what I was born to.

Images for the Season

1
pussy-willows reflected
on ripples, flutter
like bands of butterflies

2
my girl cries look
at a thin-necked robin
strained up, clearing
his throat for a song

3
a foal among
rags of april snow
spring's wobbled up to me
and nudged me
with his milky nose.

"Callum"
in memory of a novice miner

He had hair like mustard-weed;
shoulders a scoop;
eyes a lake you see the rocks on bottom;
and his voice swung a loop
with music in what it said
that tangled inside your head.

"Callum" was his name
— pronounced as if he'd sign it on the sun.
From "The Island" he came:
don't know which one.

We dropped to work in our cage,
hearts somewhere behind on a parachute.
That pusher was cute
— saw him a guy who'd count doing right important,
put him at a hard job beside a well
…a hundred and forty feet,
and he fell.

Look anywhere:
at buildings bumping on clouds,
at spider-grill bridges:
you'll see no plaque or stone for men killed there*:
    but on the late shift
the drill I'm bucking bangs his name in code
…"Callum":
though where "The Island" is I'll never know.

Gerry Galagher has since made this untrue, in one case.

Milton Acorn

The Idea

It's events itch the idea
into existence. The clawing
pixilating world lofts
the mind and its wrangling images
as contrary, gusty, circling
winds toss, flaunt the flags
(splendrous as if living) of
old duchies, unforgotten empires.

Then something palpable as voltage,
maybe a grim preacher, maybe
a wild thin man on a soapbox,
or even a character lugging
a pail and whitewash brush
(whitewash or smear it's all
a point of view) takes charge:
something you want in a way
savage or happy, takes charge:
the idea grows flesh with nerves
to feel the pain of dismemberment.

But its life is death, and life's
going back to the chewing
creation obeying just itself;
so the herded clouds, dream-beasts
in the eyes' pasture, are torn
to fall like tears, like blood.
Then the idea's more like blood,
something in time with running feet,
with typewriter, with heartbeat.

November Beach

Every step in the noise
of the ocean tumbling from the skyline
to stone frozen rippled sand
is shaken in the shaking wind.

The water of your eye freezes
in one glance outward
to the ducks racing, beaks open,
tagging, zig-zagging
amidst the bullets of spray.

Encounter

Called from marking
his measured, studied
and guessed sawcut,
the carpenter

rubs back his rusty
forelock, his eyes
groping wide from shiny
cheek-sweat as if

shaken out of a dream
while he tries to fit
his thin (always thin
to him) knowledge

into the bewilderment
of a half-described
blueprint; while
gaining presence

he lets each word,
slant of your chin,
each eyelid flicker
drip from level to level

in his brain
and be counted ...
trying to fit you too
into his pictures.

Only a Recession

After hunger
two days long,
sitting happy before
a plate of beans,

I delicately slit
each kernel with
my incisors,

let my tongue run
twitching with joy
across the texture
of the meat.

Nature

As the orange-
striped cat
hunches,
glaring down,

the pale-fluffed
nestlings
he's discovered
feel cooled
in the shadow,

and

stretch their thin
necks, heavy
heads up,
hungry
beaks open,

wide
on hinges.

January Sparrow

Two rusty wires jammed rubbing
make music in January. Look up
and on a wire between two snow-tufts
a grey puff of a sparrow's
fluffed warm in this dank wind.

January Armstrong
make the air cringe again
with a song come via your gearbox larynx
from a heart big as a diesel engine!

Poem in June

A breeze wipes creases off my forehead
and my trees lean into summer,
putting on for dresses,
day-weave,
ray-weave, sap's green nakedness.

Hushtime of the singers;
wing-time, worm-time
for the squab with its crooked neck and purse-wide beak.
(On wave-blown alfalfa, a hawk-shadow's coasting.)

As a sail fills and bounds with its business of wind,
my trees lean into summer.

Pastoral

That sudden time I heard
the pulse of song in a thrush throat
my windy visions fluttered
like snow-clouds buffeting the moon.

I was born into an ambush
of preachers, propagandists, grafters,
("Fear life and death!" "Hate and pay me!")
and tho I learned to despise them all
my dreams were of rubbish and destruction.

But that song, and the drop-notes
of a brook truckling thru log-breaks and cedars,
I came to on numb clumsy limbs
to find outside the beauty inside me.

Milton Acorn

The Retired Carpenter

Tools, grips sweat-polished,
in a dinted box, loose
at all angles,
half of them vanished.

No gripes today if
old Stan stops too often
to fire up his pipe.

The Hands

Why man, those hands, dyed
earth and tobacco brown, tough
as an old alligator suitcase, fissured
a dozen extra ways, have
a grip all courtesy, a touch
delicate and sure as a young woman's.

Knowing I Live in a Dark Age

Knowing I live in a dark age before history,
I watch my wallet and
am less struck by gunfights in the avenues
than by the newsie with his dirty pink chapped face
calling a shabby poet back for his change.

The crows mobbing the blinking, sun-stupid owl;
wolves eating a hamstrung calf hindend first,
keeping their meat alive and fresh …these
are marks of foresight, beginnings of wit:
but Jesus wearing thorns and sunstroke
beating his life and death into words
to break the rods and blunt the axes of Rome:
this and like things followed.

Knowing that in this advertising rainbow
I live like a trapeze artist with a headache,
my poems are no aspirins …they show
pale bayonets of grass waving thin on dunes;
the paralytic and his lyric secrets;
my friend Al, union builder and cynic,
hesitating to believe his own delicate poems
lest he believe in something better than himself:
and history, which is yet to begin,
will exceed this, exalt this
as a poem erases and rewrites its poet.

Death Poem

Viki's crying
over a kitten
dead
and the waters
of my brain shake.

God, what is this whisper
of Your existence?

Today the radio blared
news of Marilyn's death.
She, bold with joy
never allowing grief,
left us holding the bag
...a suicide.

I never had to believe
in God, He
believed in me
I've been sure.
Did He believe in Marilyn
and the kitten I buried?

Dead, the atoms lose
intricate jointure,
muscles clot and a
skull once washed with visions
is silent,
milk-stained lips
stiffen.

Viki's tears etch
my insides,
search me
for empty places,
unstick the walls
and open them.
I fear and question
the man I'm becoming.

House

Building forms in a mudhole
under the old man's eye,
I said, "Look up!"
at three geese scooting low.

I loved that fusty old
muttering man,
always looking, up, down,
    to the left or
    right of you.

    (He'd scan earth
    at his feet
    as if the house
    stood there,
    him figuring,
    edging,
    adjusting.)
I loved him.

So I bugged him. Told him:
"Listen to the song sparrows,
they've divvied up this property.
We're their people."
or "My balls ring
in tune with this hammer."
I wanted to see his nose
perk and take a good sniff
of the spring air;
    but knew
    sooner or later
    he'd fire me.

Milton Acorn

Offshore Breeze

The wind, heavy from the land, irons the surf
to a slosh on silver-damp sand.
The sea's grey and crocheted with ripples;
but shadows, the backs of waves,
lengthen and lapse in the dim haze,
hinting of farther, rougher doings.

The boats went out early, but now
come worm-slow thru haze and distance.
Their gunnels invisible, the men and engines
dots moving on a spit of foam,
they travel past my vision, past
that red jag of a headland, to harbour.

Lee Side in a Gale

Black sea and shone-thru sky
all mixed up along
a jumpity-jagged, beat-up
mercury saw of a skyline.

That rusty old cape hides me
but wind pokes round for me,
worries me like a scarecrow, howls
like a train from no-direction
then all-of-a-sudden whacks me.

The Schooner

Keen the tools, keen the eyes,
white the thought of the schooner
lined on a draughting board,
fine the stone that ground the fine blade
and skills, the many fingers
that stroked and touched it surely
till, intricate delicate strong
it leans poised in the wind:

The wind that has its own ways,
pushing eddying rippling invisible
in light or darkness;
now no engineer or engine
can guide you but
only the delicacy of touch against touch
underneath the breathing heaven.

I'd Like to Mark Myself

I'd like to mark myself
quiet, like one serene
calligraph in a colour
so subtle it should only
be imagined (something

like a tree in winter
bears its lines and clusters
of snow, as if what's fallen
on it were its own).

I'd like to be quiet
except for a queer grin
that tells nothing but
whatever your own want
takes it as meaning.

But if I'm ever like that
don't believe me. You'll
know that I'm kind of
like a bud …that I'm

waiting for the moment
when I can project
the tip of my tongue
and taste a raindrop

warm.

Why a Carpenter Wears His Watch
Inside the Wrist

They say it's guarded better
there, from the bumps of the trade.

I disproved this, and

guessed first those patched people
stuck up like chimneys
in high places, fix them
there so's to look at them
with no long upsetting armswing,
just a turn of the wrist,

but the gruesome truth is
that with the gargoyle-pussed
boss watching, they
don't worry much about balance;

which led me to the real reason
they wear watches tucked close
bouncing and scratching
among all their tools...

it's so they can look quick
out of the lefteyecorner
without the foreman seeing.

Poem

My mother goes in slippers
and her weight thumps the floor,
but when I think of her I think of one smile
when she was young

and to me was a goddess of green age
tho now I remember her young
with hair red as a blossom.

I remember the whole room full of that smile
and myself scampering across the edges.

Now she lives on cigarettes and wine,
goes from potted plant to flower,
knowing the time and manner
of each one's tending.

Inland Gull

Over drab-shingled peak,
skating on land-buffed air,
white as sun-fierce snow
on a great height,
white
beneath a dirty woollen sky.

His beak, a hooked pencil-mark,
scratches arrogance on brittle gusts.
A refugee from the storm,
it seems his own:
his baleful prophecy.

Hear with the Wind Still

Hear with the wind still, the grass still,
sharp and erect like animal ears,
its green darkened,
the air and its light dark green,

birds hidden in the just trembling
leaves, chirping hoarse wonder,
and one white butterfly dancing into shade
the rustle of the rain coming on.

The Ballad of the Pink-Brown Fence

Against the pink-brown fence with the sprucelet
My little sister stands to be photographed;
Fire tinges from her head and the dandelions —
Tear down the pink-brown fence to make a raft

Tear down the pink-brown fence to make a raft
Where my little sister stands to be photographed
Fish poke up their noses to make rings
And memories of dandelions dance from the ripples....

The camera is too slow to catch the gold
Of dandelions remembered around my little sister;
Stand up the old raft for a painting board
And guess the why of it — you can't recall kissing her....

Cut up the rotten painting for a bonfire;
The flames rush up a rattle, faint boom, and whisper;
Sparks fly gold in the night and then white;
Dandelions, and the hair of my little sister

Live with Me on Earth Under the Invisible Daylight Moon

Live with me on Earth among red berries and the bluebirds
And leafy young twigs whispering
Within such little spaces, between such floors of green, such
      figures in the clouds
That two of us could fill our lives with delicate wanting:

Where stars past the spruce copse mingle with fireflies
Or the dayscape flings a thousand tones of light back at the
      sun —
Be any one of the colours of an Earth lover;
Walk with me and sometimes cover your shadow with mine.

The Natural History of Elephants

In the elephant's five-pound brain
The whole world's both table and shithouse
Where he wanders seeking viandes, exchanging great farts
For compliments. The rumble of his belly
Is like the contortions of a crumpling planetary system.
Long has he roved, his tongue longing to press the juices
From the ultimate berry, large as
But tenderer and sweeter than a watermelon;
And he leaves such signs in his wake that pygmies have fallen
And drowned in his great fragrant marshes of turds.

In the elephant's five-pound brain
The wind is diverted by the draughts of his breath,
Rivers are sweet gulps, and the ocean
After a certain distance is too deep for wading.
The earth is trivial, it has the shakes
And must be severely tested, else
It'll crumble into unsteppable clumps and scatter off
Leaving the great beast bellowing among the stars.

In the elephant's five-pound brain
Dwarves have an incredible vicious sincerity,
A persistent will to undo things. The beast cannot grasp
The convolutions of destruction, always his mind
Turns to other things — the vastness of green
And of frangibility of forest. If only once he could descend
To trivialities he'd sweep the whole earth clean of his tormentors
In one sneeze so mighty as to be observed from Mars.

In the elephant's five-pound brain
Sun and moon are the pieces in a delightfully complex ballgame
That have to do with him ...never does he doubt
The sky has opened and rain and thunder descend
For his special ministration. He dreams of mastodons

And mammoths and still his pride beats
Like the heart of the world, he knows he could reach
To the end of space if he stood still and imagined the effort.

In the elephant's five-pound brain
Poems are composed as a silent substitute for laughter,
His thoughts while resting in the shade
Are long and solemn as novels and he knows his companions
By names differing for each quality of morning.
Noon and evening are ruminated on and each overlaid
With the taste of night. He loves his horny perambulating hide
As other tribes love their houses, and remembers
He's left flakes of skin and his smell
As a sign and permanent stamp on wherever he has been.

In the elephant's five-pound brain
The entire Oxford dictionary'ld be too small
To contain all the concepts which after all are too weighty
Each individually ever to be mentioned;
Thus of course the beast has no language
Only an eternal pondering hesitation.

In the elephant's five-pound brain
The pliable trunk's a continuous diversion
That in his great innocence he never thinks of as perverse,
The pieces of the world are handled with such a thrilling
Tenderness that all his hours
Are consummated and exhausted with love.
Not slow to mate every female bull and baby
Is blessed with a gesture grandly gracious and felt lovely
Down to the sensitive great elephant toenails.

And when his more urgent pricking member
Stabs him on its horrifying season he becomes
A blundering mass of bewilderment .... No thought
But twenty tons of lust he fishes madly for whales
And spiders for copulation. Sperm falls in great gouts
And the whole forest is sticky, colonies of ants
Are nourished for generations on dried elephant semen.

In the elephant's five-pound brain
Death is accorded no belief and old friends
Are continually expected, patience
Is longer than the lives of glaciers and the centuries
Are rattled like toy drums. A life is planned
Like a brushstroke on the canvas of eternity,
And the beginning of a damnation is handled
With great thought as to its middle and its end.

Apple Tree in the Wind

Which is the sun and which is the wind
Sweeping like a yellow broom?
The shadow of my garage — called a studio
By my mother, who must confer me dignity
Creeps with its gable like a spearpoint....

And now its point is lost it tosses
A whole head of shadow-plumes
Borrowed from another tree;
Softened before it reaches the apple-tree —

Where the wind waves leaf-fans
Covering one red apple-face
To open another .... Red balls
Ready to bounce into the mouths of children;
Or maybe if I'm not too lazy
Into applesauce, made by my mother:
The stove is waiting and humming: —

It's the Last Stormtime

It's the last stormtime of winter. As if the ghosts of ancestors
Forgetting even they are ancestors
Were wandering. They cannot groan so the trees groan for
  them;
The hiss of the snows is their wordless breath.

Survivors they were who hunted survivors
The stumbling moose, the slumbering bear, the rabbit…
Always winter was the season of their wanderings
And now they wander like fragmented crystals of snow.

It's the last stormtime, when summer seems a fantasy,
Something dreamt of, a visit to another planet.
Gawd I feel I was an oversize dumptruck
Loaded with everything that fell this year;
All the snow, all the soot and debris in it.

Somewhere else, in both space and time,
The snow's cleaner, but no less fierce.
Now when even the dullest eye looks up for the faintest hint
  or hope of blue;
When it's unthinkable that winter once was pleasant;
Now's the thing like a moment when somewhere, somewhen
The ancestors are wandering; cold, hunger, tiredness,
The void in the head where there should be memory — all
  these are the same.

They must slay the great beast of spring
Whose decay is a field of berries, whose decay is the one-eyed
  sun
In whose yellow lashes all colours revive
And the living remember who they were
So the dead perhaps may remember too.

The Second World War

Down Great George Street, up to the station;
The skirl of the pipes the very thrill of your nerves
With the pipemaster (only man who has the Gaelic)
Ahead with his great baton, his strut and toss proud
    as any man who's ever walked.
This is where we came in; this has happened before
Only the last time there was cheering.
So few came back they changed the name of the regiment
So there're no cheers now. Tho there are crowds
Standing silent, eyes wide as dolls' eyes, but brighter
Trying to memorize every face

This is where we came in. It happened before.
    The last time was foolishness
Now's got to be done because of the last foolishness.
In the ranks, perfectly in step (with the pipes
    even I'm perfectly in step)
I'm thinking of *Through the Looking Glass*:
The White King's armies marching while he sleeps;
We are his dream…. At least it seems that way.
They're so clumsy the front line topples
The second line topples over it; and on it goes
    — line after line, eyes glazed straight forward
Shoulders back, spines held stiffly unnatural
Toppling over the line before

So few came back they abolished the regiment.
I was lucky — sickness and bad marksmanship.
Man by man we'd sworn to take our guns back,
    man by man we didn't.
One man — one war — that's all he's usually good for.
Now a strange short-haired subculture
Glares at us out of the TV set
Snarling the news, every phrase or disguised opinion
    as if it was a threat, which it is.
This is where we came in
It's happened before.
This last time was right
But ended in foolishness.
It has happened before, could happen again
Despite the fact that stuff is out of date.

The Sea

Limitless sea? A lie! The sea's limited
To a variousness — nothing it's ever been can be
      repeated.
The light striking the water now, here, an hour before
      sunset
Makes it the colour of a pale Chinese ink
But such a precise shade of Chinese ink has never
      existed
Nor will any part of the sea be that precise shade again.

Infinity and finitude play loop-the-loop.
The sea, in every moment of all its ages
Has been different from anything it's been
And different from anything it'll ever be.
Repetition is impossible — no painting, no matter how
      truly
It catches the rage, the play, the calm of the sea
Is anything like the sea can possibly be
Yet there's no limit to its possibility
Even tho there're things the sea can never be.

No wave can ever duplicate another. The wavelets,
The weaving cross-hatches on the great waves
Can never cover one wave as they cover another;
The droplet of spray never flies from the same place
(how could you fix it as the same place?)
It rises. It roars. Like monstrous teeth
Its sudden upflingings threaten the atmosphere which
      torments it:
And its colours change, its loops and traps change.
      It'll never be the same.

Milton Acorn

The Big Saw

Many's the time when I was on the job
The sawman came to me:
"You're able — and you can work fast.
Why don't you handle the big saw?"

Upon which I'd hold up my hands
Thumbs and fingers spread out:
"Look. Count 'em. Ten, isn't there?
That's how many there's going to be!"

I, Milton Acorn
after Brecht

I, Milton Acorn, not at first aware
That was my name and what I knew was life,
Come from an Island to which I've often returned
Looking for peace, and usually found strife.

till I came to see it was no pocket
In a saint's pants while outside trouble reigned;
And after all my favourite mode
Of weather's been a hurricane.

The spattered colour of the time has marked me
So I'm a man of many appearances;
Have come many times to poetry
And come back to define what was meant.

Often I've been coupled, and often alone
No matter how I try I can't choose
Which it shall be. I've been
Ill-treated, but often marvellously well-used.

What's a man if not put to good use?
Nothing's happened I want to forget.
What's a day without a notable
Event between sunrise and sunset?

My present lover finds me gentle
So gentle I'll be in my boisterous way.
Another one was heard to call me noble.
That didn't stop her from going away.

To be born on an island's to be sure
You are native with a habitat.
Growing up on one's good training
For living in a country, on a planet.

Shall I tell you the soil's red
As a flag? Sand a pink flesh gleam
You could use to tone a precious stone?
All its colours are the colours of dreams.

Perhaps only the colours *I* dream
For I grew under that prismatic sky
Like a banner of many colours
Alternately splashed and washed clean.

The Island's small ...Every opinion counts.
I'm accustomed to fighting for them.
Lord I thank Thee for the enemies
Who even in childhood tempered me.

I beg pardon, God, for the insult
Saying You lived and were responsible
...a tortuous all-odds-counting manner
Of thinking marks me an Islander.

Evil's been primary, good secondary
In the days I've been boy, youth and man.
I don't look to any rule of pure virtue
But certainly not continuance of this damned....

Damned! Damned did I say? This glorious age
When the ancient rule of classes is hit
And hit again. History's greatest change
Is happening ...And I'm part of it.

William Cooper

Who knows William Cooper. Who gives a damn?
Was his hair black or fair or red?
How many bullets whizzed past his head?
How did their number compare with the number of the hairs,
Or was he bald and the bullets outnumber the hairs?

How many times did he aim his musket
In threat? How many times did he fire it?
Always to warn and miss or sometimes to hit?
Who knows William Cooper? Who gives a damn?
Who wants to remember that old war?
How many claim him for ancestor?

I see him bald. That's my fancy
With beard like a tongue licking from Hell
To sizzle the landlords and their agents;
Eyes the steel of the sea on a cold calm day;
Though they might like mine be Indian brown
...Indian eyes that see the soul
And never notice a tuft of hay
Toss without wondering *"What made it bend that way?"*

William Cooper's part of the history
Of Prince Edward Island — Canadian history, therefore
Officially blank; but forbidden history
Is still history; We react and think
According to our history
Even though we may not know it.

Except our actions are slower, confused
And since our history's been misused
Old mistakes are often repeated.

I've been told his voice when it roared
Was heard seven miles downriver, sometimes more.
All the steeples in Charlottetown swayed
And letter bags to London were filled
As if at the puff of his words and breath.

"Send us troops …Troops!" Those letters implored
And usually the answers, after all consideration
Wavered and swayed
Back across the ocean to say:
"How many troops did we send you before?
And now you tell us they all deserted!
Do you think Victoria in all her majesty
Is going to wage a major campaign
Against Prince Edward Island?
Empires have been felled by troops, felled by ships
Empires have been knocked down by earthquakes;
And we don't want to be knocked down
By any earthquake of laughter!"

Who knows William Cooper? Who gives a damn?
Was he a giant or a small man?
Often he bounced with energy, stood long in
meditation;
Argued passionately, argued patiently;
Moved among the venom eyes of his enemies
Because the eyes of his friends were there too
Watchful as God is said to watch
And a hawk watches for sartin.

John Dhru Macintosh Stands Up in Church
(Saint Margaret's: 1844)

Young John MacDonald …Father as yer called:
A curse it be upon yer father's name
That you bear the same.
                      Landlord and priest!
Did the shaggy fiend I see standing ahind ye
Think up that combination?
Or was it yersel' since I never knew him
Except thru watching you and yer action.

What a fine life ye hae, coming round
Wi' one a yer claws stretched out fer rent
An' the other one fer tithes,
Hearing confessions! How can we
ever get to own our own land
wi' you onto all our secrets?
Now as the scripture says
We've all took our heads an' reasoned together.

Figured we paid ye enough an' more
For any sacrifice yer father made
an' declare the land is ours: but
we'll hae mercy upon ye.
Gae ye the chance t' make up fer all yer sins.
Take up all yer gear an' leave this parish
Or be a martyr…

Dragging for Traps

When you're hanging to a pendulum
you wouldn't be there unless there's something to do
so mind the swing and mind your job;
like when you're out in a lobster boat
dragging for traps in the swell after the storm.
No time to think: "What am I
doing here, whose mother
loved me along with other fools?"

Turn into the waves and toss,
turn to the side and roll 45 degrees plus,
turn your back to them and mind the splash.
Just don't think you're going to be seasick.
All the time there's traps on the shore
bumped, bruised, broken, tangled with their lines.
Hold on and drag, trying not to be sure
that they're the very traps you're dragging for.

The Squall

When the squall comes running down the bay,
Its waves like hounds on slanting leashes of rain
Bugling their way…and you're in it;
If you want more experience at this game
Pull well and slant well. Your aim
Is another helping of life. You've got to win it.

When you're caught in an eight-foot boat — seaworthy
      though —
You've got to turn your back, for a man rows backwards
Taking direction from the sting of rain and spray.
How odd, when you think of it, that a man rows backwards!

How odd, when you think of it, that a man rows backwards.
What experience, deduction and sophistication
There had to be before men dared row backwards
Taking direction from where they'd been
With only quick-snatched glances at where they're going.

Each strongbacked wave bucks under you, alive
Young-muscled, wanting to toss you in orbit
While whitecaps snap like violin-strings
As if to end this scene with a sudden exit.

Fearfulness is a danger. So's fearlessness.
You've got to get that mood which balances you
As if you were a bird in the builder's hand;
For the boat was built in consideration
Not only of storms …of gales too.

Milton Acorn

Though you might cut the waves with your prow
It'll do no good if you head straight to sea.
You've got to make a nice calculation
Of where you're going, where you want to be,
What you need, and possibility;
Remembering how you've survived many things
To get into the habit of living.

Incident from the Land Struggle (1767–1873)

"Well sirs, then we're agreed on the plan.
Black John here will fire on this Englishman
And miss (make sure of that, lad
The battle depends on this)
One quarter mile on, White John
Will miss too, but closer, and if that
Stinking piece of rent-collecting manure
Who dares call himself a gentleman
Keeps on, Red John will shoot his horse.
Old John here will then happen along
And lend him his horse — the red stallion.
Once he's on that beast, no more worries
Except to collect the remains, living or dead
And carry them back to Charlottetown
And, of course demand our expenses
Be very particularly
                    angry
                            about that."

That Corrugated Look to Water

That corrugated look to water
— grey with a glitter:
I've been told now that it's ice;
microscopic bergs clashing,
making music of many thin tones
too faint for us to hear.

Gulls fly labouring
low and straight, point to point;
bouncing off air pressed down
by their own wingbeats,
tips walking on
the same wingtips reflected.

No day this for men
to be at business on the water
— no longer ours, but winter's.
Wind's so raw you don't know if
you're freezing or boiling;

though there are no waves, only
winking, glittering
ripples flittering against
downthrusting cold chunks
of air. We glimpse
it from the land through chinks
between hills, trees, houses;
and eyes ache
with brief sightings of
light shooting
flying needle
-icicle rays.

The Figure in the Landscape
Made the Landscape

The figure in the landscape made the landscape
Like the farmer you see in this painting I've imagined
Pre-Confederation, pre
Any moment you might wish to be in or not
Since the loyalists came, instantized themselves into
rebels
Or when they were joined, reinforced by Scottish
clansmen.

His beard may be like a sprucetree upside down
Or scraggy from recent Indian mixture;
But whatever his eyecolour was a moment before;
Preoccupied with work, keen with observation,
Wild in a laugh or soft and genial;
Now the man invisible in the picture
As the painter's invisible but still there;
The landlord's agent sees nothing but hellfire.

"Ye'll get no rent for woods ye didn't cut,
Stumps dug out with a horse I had to borrow,
Land I ploughed — me and my old lady
Who wasn't so old those days — me in harness
And her at the handles;

A road I made with friends and relatives;
And the wharf. When's there goin'ta be a wharf here?
Don't bother with that. We'll manage without ye
As well as we'll manage without payin' rent."

Except four things I'll mention later
Everything he wears or carries
Is his own — right from the sheep's back
It was made by him or his kin, even the dye
Whose base, if you want to know, spouted from his body.

Milton Acorn

Four things were bought or obtained otherwise
...his hat (tho he himself trapped the beaver
His boots tho it's himself grew slaughtered and skinned
        the beast, tanned the leather;
And the musket past which his hellfire eyes glare.

Of course he saw the agent coming
If not as usual warned long in advance. He's never worked
        long
Anytime in his life with his head always down.
Always straightened for thirty seconds every five minutes
To scan the landscape for any strange object,
And as a vacation for maybe five seconds
Bathing in its beauty like it was his own sweat.
Islanders to this day retain this habit.

And the landscape rolling like a quilt
By one of those strange fitnesses
Of geography and history
Is red and green, red and green, two rebellious colours;
Clearings and woodlots, clearings and woodlots:
Seldom even today is an entire farm cleared
As woodlots made the land difficult
To spy out, for anyone not familiar with the place,
And besides that make good ambuscades.

Today the tourists, pawns who don't know they're
Pawns in a new still-just-brooding
Struggle for the land, skim past
Or poke around slow wondering
At the beauty and gentleness
Of the Island countryside, the Island people
(those who fight best are kind to each other)
With every turn in the road a new surprise.
Few of them think that's the way it was designed.
"A lovely land," they say, "and peaceful"
When every part of it was laid out for war.

If You're Stronghearted
after Auden

If you're stronghearted look at this Island;
red gouges of creeks at low tide and
the stronger red which spreads behind ploughs.
Don't hold your tongue too long, it'll swell
with so much good and so much bad to say.

If you're stronghearted look at the clouds
growing and raising heads to look themselves,
opening mouths to say what should be said.

If you're stronghearted ripple your way
up and down over low green-patched hills.
You can look from twenty feet and be unobserved
except for the fire of your eyes.
Strong eyes …they've seen such beauty
that a nerve runs from each to the heart.

If you're stronghearted put your ear to the ground
to hear the lilt and cut of soft voices
discussing enemy moves without fear.

The Stormbirds

In a storm the dull gulls flock inland.
The tern, the gallant tern makes out to sea;
Tacking, slanting against a forty-knot wind
To where the action is, and plumb shifts
Like hands of a clock with springs gone wild;
Fishing at their best where nothing stays pinned;
Swirling in flocks like snow upon green drifts:
Like a mind never at rest, they are at rest.

Realisant souls are the souls solidly
Set in these unsolid worlds and spaces.
With everything restless, nothing staying just so;
I keep in this eternal state of fission:
Back from a mission, off towards a mission;
Simultaneously I return and go.

Island Moon

The moon's a dime worn out of round;
Clear stare from a one-eyed captain's tomcat;
Fountain spraying with clear hard pale cider
This rolling land with half-abandoned orchards
Too small today to be kept for sound
Countable profit, culled for other rewards.

Who has named these colours of the moon;
Given to this pasture, that oatfield, those slight
Poplars like shivering-on-one-leg sentries
With short tartans wrapped round them tight?
The road down to the untraceably gone shipyard
Was dug deep once to make do for a trench;
And the river's glittering like a silver fork
Once stuck hard in the land, hefted and bent.

Milton Acorn

The Wake-Up Raven

A most unghostly whistle, like a toy
Factory's — at the dim brown hour of four
Angled down from those ponderously stirred
Trees near the heaving, hunching slowpoke waves;
Used to shake me quick from dreams to wonder:
Till I knew it had to be a raven
Waking his relatives to plunder
Breakfast in this first, best, worst hour of war.

Now it's all routine, I'm up and to work
At a craft not the canniest raven knows
With half an ear for panic in the forest
Where they as well raise hell and drive blows.
Such quirks in my beloved reality:
The cruelest time for raven-work's best for me.

Invocation

You loved one, hurt one, loving one still strong …
If you were only an impossible vision
Why would you lurk — a quiet worm in my tongue
Wait and live to raise this invocation?
What did you look through, in Spook Canyon
Besides that smiling mask, carved from a tree —
Tools learning as they cut a growing wisdom
To top and ornament your poor wronged body?
You have entered me, dead but not done.

I've loved, and love the Earth. If you are Death
Stay around to summon more performance.
Is that smile kinder yet? Plumbing consent?
Wait for the laughter! It'll blow breath
Tumbling all your atoms to collect 'em
Til lungs pump, your heart flutters, eyes go wide
And I'll be wise, at last, to find a bride.
My vehicle accelerates, bright one. Come.

Miracle with One Witness

"Poetry and sainthood ought to be
The aspiration of a man or woman,
Or they should ply some instrument at least —
I'm serious," said Captain Neal MacDougal.
"I myself used to manipulate the
Juice harp as I was brought up to call it
Before I found that talking was my bent.
I was meant to be a saint but worked too hard."

Seen by him alone, a being appeared
Who had the manner and grace of a woman
A teasing look that challenged and afeared.
She stuck out a tongue to lick his whole head
Totally around, inward through his brain:
"Say what you can although your task's insane."

Captain Neal MacDougal
and The Naked Goddess

"She rubs some heavenly oil upon her body
So as never to be in need of clothes,
Which she might wear nevertheless
Since truth is variable. She is the female
God of truth; therefore goes in nudity:
Might for a lesson shuffle out of flesh
To show off her becoming skeleton
In marvelous clitter-and-clatter capers,
Or might be only wind as her own clothes;
Or might indeed put on a man for dress…
Thus the idea that our God's a male"
Said Captain Neal MacDougal, but the fright
In those awed listener's eyes clappered tight
His lips into an unconscious grave smile.

MacDougal's Vision of Ocean

A herringbone pattern runs on the sea
Over-billowing depths and silences;
Depths and noises, such a cacophony
Of busy clatter about businesses
In life and death, nutrition, excrement:
It gives a man the bothers just to think…
Such involvement in what's not much meant
Down where krakens grab and serpents slink.

The ripples move in heavy undulation
Above all that, where all things undulate
With not much time to sleep or take vacations;
No more than a poet can duck his fate
Of blowing ruffled billows, shuffling words:
Or fishermen from fishing fishy herds.

Anne Compton

The Completion of the Fiddle
(N.M.)

The fiddle's incomplete without the dance;
My darling. Let's hook fingers to complete
By motion to the calls, the sweet riddle
Of the tune now wriggling in the soft wind
On top of which the bright moon goes riding;
For if no happy bottoms prance and spin
Upon the planks and polish what's it all worth —
That round of steamed, shaped, rehardened wood
Varnished as it's put about a hollow
From which a tune may radiate its mirth
By the merry rub of gut against gut?
The candles flicker and the stars twinkle
All to be parts of the completed fiddle!

Milton Acorn

Island Farm

Rankle-hearted jay, why are you scolding
Me working in my own field?
Perhaps you think the land's not mine?
Maybe she isn't, it's been in the family
For generations I'd count if I took the time;
On some occasions been well peopled
With other sweaty men, mostly neighbours
And just now much of this machinery
Isn't mine. It's borrowed. Or will be lent
Since we must take care of each other
Whilst counting every dollar made or spent.

Curse his soul! Here comes the sheriff
With all his threats remarkably similar
To ones such another made to my great-great-grandfather.... .

Anne Compton

Those Country Guys

Those guys with wart-hard faces
gouged like an old field,
never took a holiday
on the date revealed
by red figures on the calendar
timidly appealed for
by the sometimes fierce legislature.

Mind you they weren't scared!
When the boss (an old hand himself
wistful for a day to spend
with a pipe, a pint of rum, and argument
asked round, they told him
if he cared
to grin away a day they'd
manage without him —
meanwhile they talked so much
of wives, relatives and broods,
I felt shrivelled by their virtues.

So I heaved and hammered
beside them all spring;
but when the yellow sun-glint
skipped the waves of summer,
began to see absences.
Each with a good excuse:
"The calves are loose
in the swamp — my well's dry,
we've got to witch for water"
...jobs alike in this way:
they took all day.

But with the autumn clouds tall
mirrored on their eyeballs,
the sky trailed like smoke with migrants,
they said, "We're after ducks
tomorrow. If that ain't liked
this job'll be over.
What the hell's life for?"
Those country guys lazed
at the right times, namely
when they damn pleased.

Poem

My soul's no white wind-balanced gull.
It's a wolverine
...a bounce-and-hobble poke-and-punch
hunchback dangerous snuffling thing
whose salvation's the taste of the moment.

I'm the wobbly deep-eyed fawn, its prey
harried forever back into childhood
away from certainties
the eyes know and find
to cancel the tossy-clouded sky
and all such irrelevancies.

What a hot thirst it has!
For blood, the blood of battle
Where the flesh endures its sorrows
For its high joys and agonies!

And we came from the sea, we were swept to the shore,
And we cling to the land like our ancestors before,
And we work with the nets, and we work with the plough
As the seasons pass and the centuries bow

And we came from the sea.

> — Milton Acorn & Cedric Smith,
> *The Road to Charlottetown*

Books by Milton Acorn

In Love and Anger, 1956
The Brain's the Target, 1960
Against a League of Liars, 1960
58 Poems by Milton Acorn: Fiddlehead Special Issue, 1963
Jawbreakers, 1963
I've Tasted My Blood: Poems 1956 to 1968, 1969
More Poems for People, 1972
The Island Means Minago, 1975
Jackpine Sonnets, 1977
Captain Neal MacDougal & the Naked Goddess, 1982
Dig Up My Heart: Selected Poems 1952-83, 1983

Books published posthumously

Whiskey Jack, 1986
A Stand of Jackpine: Two Dozen Canadian Sonnets, with James Deahl, 1987
The Uncollected Acorn, edited by James Deahl, 1987
I Shout Love and Other Poems, edited by James Deahl, 1987
Hundred Proof Earth, edited by James Deahl, 1988
To Hear the Faint Bells, selected by James Deahl, 1996

Drama

The Road to Charlottetown: A Play by Milton Acorn & Cedric Smith, edited by James Deahl, 1998

Index by Title

About the cover

Portrait of Milton Acorn, 1986, oil on canvas (45" x 37"), by Brian Burke, is the third in a series of portraits Burke painted of his friend Milton Acorn in the 1980s. Brian Burke lives with his wife Judith Scherer-Burke at Dalvay-by-the-Sea, Prince Edward Island. His paintings can be found in art galleries and private collections across North America and Europe.

Anne Compton

About the type

The body text for this book is set in *Electra*,
created in 1935 by William Addison Dwiggins.

—

Headlines are set in FB *Hermes*,
designed by Matthew Butterick in 1995.

Milton Acorn

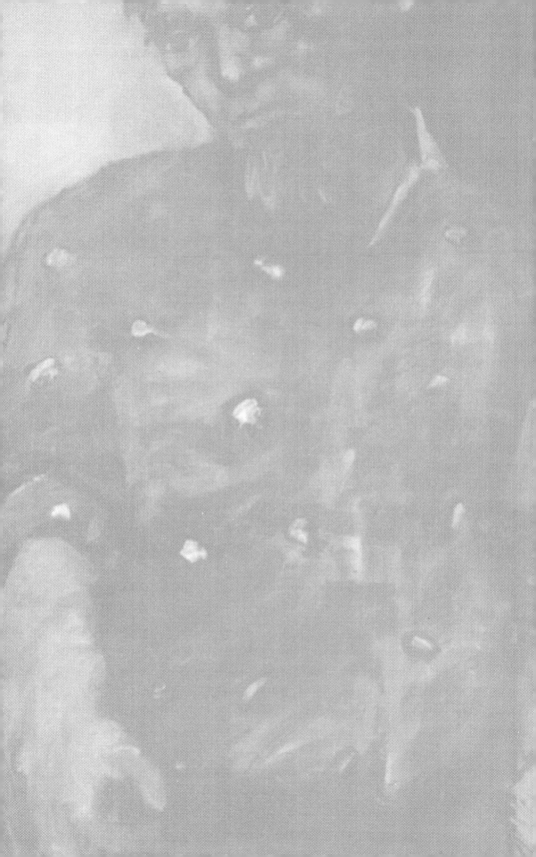